HISTORIC

CONCORD

&

THE LEXINGTON FIGHT

The Monument of 1836, and across the Bridge the "Minute Man"

HISTORIC CONCORD

*A Handbook of its Story and
its Memorials with an Account of*
THE LEXINGTON FIGHT

By Allen French

REVISED BY DAVID B. LITTLE

*Containing a revised and expanded Guide section to the
Historical and Literary sites of Lexington and Concord*

with The Friends of the Concord Free Public Library
Gambit, IPSWICH
1978

Acknowledgements

The Concord Free Public Library has both friends and Friends to maintain its broad range of services in these times of increasing costs and limited tax support. All of the Friends are friends, but not all of the friends are Friends. This new and revised edition of Allen French's HISTORIC CONCORD has been prepared, and most of its publication costs have been paid by generous friends without whom this revision would not have appeared. The proceeds from its sales go to the Library.

The "Friends of the Concord Free Public Library" are a small group organized and incorporated to provide regular volunteer assistance to the Library staff and to plan and manage such fund-raising events as the annual Friends' Book Sale. They provided the impetus needed to bring this edition of HISTORIC CONCORD from dream to reality.

We are grateful to David B. Little for rewriting the Guide section of the text, to Thompson R. Harlow, Director of The Connecticut Historical Society, and to George T. Goodspeed, Director of Goodspeed's Book Shop, Inc., for permission to publish the reproductions made by the Meriden Gravure Company for Goodspeed's Book Shop, Inc., from the original set of Doolittle prints owned by The Connecticut Historical Society. We are grateful to Bruce Lasting of Lexington and to Keith Martin of Concord for permission to publish their superb color photographs of the Lexington Minute Man and the Concord Battleground. Maps are an essential ingredient in any guide book. Sam Abbott drew these maps for us. We are most grateful to her.

Acknowledgements

We are grateful also to Paul Brooks of Lincoln, distinguished author, editor, and historian, and to the historians of the Minute Man National Historical Park for their careful reading of the text and for the improvements they have suggested. Morgan K. Smith and the staff of Gambit have earned our thanks for their skill and care in producing and publishing this book.

Most of all, we are grateful that Concord has, and has had for over a century, a public library good enough to transform its patrons into friends who support it. When William Munroe learned of the time and effort Ralph Waldo Emerson was spending on the improvement of the old town library — 7,000 volumes, open one afternoon and one evening a week — he resolved to give the town a library worthy of Mr. Emerson's attention, and, in 1873, he did. Friends have worked to keep it worthy ever since. We are proud to be numbered among them.

Charles A. S. Heinle, President
Friends of the Concord Free Public Library

Foreword

to

the 1942 Edition

Modern wars have turned the thoughts of Americans to the history of their country, rousing the desire to see not merely its famous places, but particularly those where our national spirit has been most prominently revealed. After the First World War this was proved in historic Concord by the stream of visitors who came to see the North Bridge, where Americans first marched against the British who till that moment had been their fellow citizens. These pilgrim tourists found another interest in Concord, because of the famous authors who lived there, who were among the first to give permanent expression to American literary ability. In their period equally famous American writers lived elsewhere; but as a literary group Emerson, Thoreau, Hawthorne, and the Alcotts are unsurpassed in our history. The Second World War is turning the minds of our countrymen still more seriously to Concord's evidences of our national achievements. There is every reason to believe that, once the limitations to travel are lifted, in future the visitors to Concord will be more numerous than ever.

For the convenience of such visitors this handbook has been written in two sections, a Guide and a History. As most tourists arrive in the town with little knowledge of how to see it, or with limited time at their disposal, the Guide section has been put first. The History could not be combined with it; but it should be read beforehand by those who have the leisure, and may be reviewed on reaching home. As a handbook the slight occasional repetitions are necessary, and the cross-references should be helpful.

Foreword
to
the Revised Edition

Our world has greatly changed since Allen French wrote this little handbook in 1942. Concord and Lexington have changed along with it; hence this revision of the Guide section of his text. The History section remains unchanged. unchanged.

New highways make access to Lexington and Concord easier for visitors traveling by automobile or sightseeing bus. Public transportation has declined in quality, extent, and frequency of service. The greatest change, however, has come as a result of the intervention of the federal government through the agencies of the National Park Service and the Fish and Wildlife Service, both of them functions of the U.S. Department of the Interior.

We will begin our Guide section, therefore, not at Monument Square in Concord as Allen French did, but at the National Park Service's Battle Road Visitor Center located on Route 2-A in Lexington about half a mile west of Route 128. We will expand our coverage of Lexington to match Mr. French's account of the events which took place in that town on April 19, 1775, and also to include the splendid new Museum of Our National Heritage, sponsored by the Scottish Rite of Freemasonry in the Northern

Masonic Jurisdiction of the U.S.A. We will omit a listing of open hours and admission fees for the historic houses, as they are constantly changing. The latest word is always available at the Visitor Centers in both towns.

If we are successful in this venture, Allen French's little gem will be as useful to a tourist today as it was to a visitor during the 1940s. We will welcome all suggestions for its further improvement from those who use it.

David B. Little

Introductory Note

The first violent blows of the War of the American Revolution were struck in Lexington and Concord, Massachusetts, on April 19, 1775. A detachment of British troops, on its way to Concord with orders to find and destroy military stores concealed there, killed eight of Captain Parker's company of Lexington Minute Men drawn up in formation on Lexington Green beside the road. The British troops then marched on to Concord, seized the two bridges over the rivers dividing the town, and began their search. Three of their companies holding the North Bridge fired upon minute men advancing upon it. Their fire was returned. "We have no need to magnify the facts," Ralph Waldo Emerson declared in his address at the centennial celebration in 1875. "Only two of our men were killed at the bridge, and four others wounded. But here the British army was first fronted, and driven back; and if only two men, or only one man, had been slain, it was the first victory. The thunderbolt falls on an inch of ground; but the light of it fills the horizon."

The British retreat began in a shocked silence. Fighting broke out again at Meriam's Corner and continued with increasing intensity all the way to Charlestown. The heaviest fighting occurred in the town of Arlington, then called Menotomy, where died more than half of all the combatants killed during this, the first day of the War of the American Revolution.

During the two centuries which separate us from this historic event, the Battle Road has continued to be a public highway, at first one of the few, now one of the many, linking Lexington and Concord with the city of Boston. It has been repeatedly widened, straightened, paved, drained, lighted, and equipped with traffic signals. Within the perimeter of Massachusetts Route 128, its borders have been cleared of ancient dwellings and filled with the many kinds of structures needed by the expanding cities and towns along the way. Much of this change has occurred during the past fifty years.

We are indebted to the Arlington Historical Society for its rescue of the Jason Russell house, where the owner and eleven minute men died in hand-to-hand combat with British troops, whose casualties were also heavy. The house now stands at 7 Jason Street near Massachusetts Avenue just west of Arlington center.

We are indebted also to the town of Lexington for preserving its Common, frequently called Lexington Green, and to the Lexington Historical Society for the three historic houses it preserves and displays so well. Little else of the Revolutionary period remains along the Battle Road between Route 128 and Boston.

From Route 128 to Concord, however, enough of the old road has survived to make possible its re-creation from Fiske Hill in Lexington to Meriam's Corner in Concord. Realizing that it was only a matter of time before this, too, would disappear under modern development, historians and other interested citizens applied pressure on the Congress of the United States. The Boston National Historic Sites Commission was appointed by the Congress in 1955 "to make a study of historic sites, buildings, and objects in Boston and the vicinity thereof relating to the Colonial and Revolutionary period of American history. The purpose of this study is to recommend the role that the Federal Government, local, and State governmental bodies, and historical and patriotic societies should undertake with regard to the future preservation of these properties."

The *Interim Report of the Boston National Historic Sites Commission Pertaining to the Lexington-Concord Battle Road* was published in 1959 as House Document No. 57, 86th

Congress, 1st Session. In accordance with its recommendations, by act of Congress, September 21, 1959, the establishment of the Minute Man National Historical Park was authorized "in order to preserve for the benefit of the American people certain historic structures and properties of outstanding national significance associated with the opening of the War of the American Revolution."

Re-creation of the old road has been delayed by the inability of the Commonwealth of Massachusetts and the towns through which it passes to agree on a new location for Route 2-A between Route 128 and Concord. Nevertheless, with its land acquisitions nearly completed, the Minute Man National Historical Park was formally established, and the Battle Road Visitor Center dedicated, on May 8, 1976.

The park also owns and controls the land surrounding the Old North Bridge in Concord. The road from Monument Street to the bridge and the knoll on which "The Minute Man" statue stands continue to be the property of the town of Concord, but it is operated by the National Park Service under the terms of a cooperative agreement. The land in Concord bordering the Battle Road between Meriam's Corner and the Battleground at the Old North Bridge has been designated by the town as one of several Historic Districts in the town.

Contents

Acknowledgments   vii

Foreword to the 1942 edition   ix

Foreword to the revised edition   xi

INTRODUCTORY NOTE   xiii

    ROAD MAP TO THE BATTLE ROAD
    VISITOR CENTER FROM ROUTES
    2 AND 128   xxii

GUIDE: Where to begin a visit to
Lexington and Concord   1

    The Battle Road Visitor Center   1
    THE LEXINGTON MINUTEMAN   following 2

GUIDE to Lexington: Routes for the tourist
to follow in seeing the principal sights   3

    Lexington Green   3
    Map of Lexington Center   following 3
    Buckman Tavern   4
    Revolutionary Monument   4
    Lexington Visitors Center   5
    Hancock-Clarke House   5
    Cary Memorial Building   6
    Munroe Tavern   6
    Sanderson House   7
    Museum of Our National Heritage   8
    Fiske Hill, Fiske Farm   8

GUIDE to Concord: Routes for the tourist to follow in seeing the principal sights

GUIDE to Concord: Routes for the tourist
to follow in seeing the principal sights   11

GUIDE TO CONCORD, GENERAL   11
  Map of Concord   following 11

THE SQUARE   12

  Colonial Inn   13
  Wright Tavern   15
  Hill Burying Ground   15

MONUMENT STREET   17

  House with the Bullet Hole   18
  Old Manse   18
  Battleground   20

CONCORD BATTLEGROUND   following 22

  Major John Buttrick House and Monument 25
  North Bridge Visitor Center   25

*LOWELL ROAD AND BARRETT'S
  MILL ROAD*   26

  Old Calf Pasture   26
  Barrett's Mill   27
  Barrett's Farm   27

BEDFORD STREET   27

  Sleepy Hollow Cemetery   28
  Great Meadows National Wildlife Refuge 30

MAIN STREET (THE MILLDAM)   31

  *South Quarter, or Main Street, Burying
    Ground*   32
  Public Library   32
  Concord Academy   33
  Thoreau-Alcott House   33
  Franklin B. Sanborn House   33
  South Bridge Boat House   34

Joseph Hosmer House and Hosmer Cottage   34
Thoreau Lyceum   34

WALDEN POND   35

Thoreau's house at Walden   36

LEXINGTON ROAD   38

First Parish Church, Concord Art
    Association, Reuben Brown House   38
Emerson House   40
Concord Museum (Concord Antiquarian Society) 40
Orchard House   42
School of Philosophy   44
Wayside   44
Grapevine Cottage   46
Meriam's Corner   46
Thoreau's Birthplace   47

HISTORY: A brief study of the first two
hundred and fifty years, 1635-1885   48

THE COLONIAL PERIOD   48

Topography   48
The Founding   49
King Philip's War   51
Governor Andros   52

THE REVOLUTIONARY PERIOD   53

Preparations   53
Lexington   56
Concord   60

The Doolittle Prints of the Battles
of Lexington and Concord   following   70

Concord in Literature   73

Emerson   74

Bronson Alcott	80
Louisa Alcott	83
Thoreau	84
Hawthorne	88
Other Writers	91

Bibliography   93

Index   99

Illustrations by Lester G. Hornby, Amos Doolittle, Harry C. Fenn, Bruce Lasting, and Keith T. Martin

Maps by Sam Abbott

HISTORIC

CONCORD

&

THE LEXINGTON FIGHT

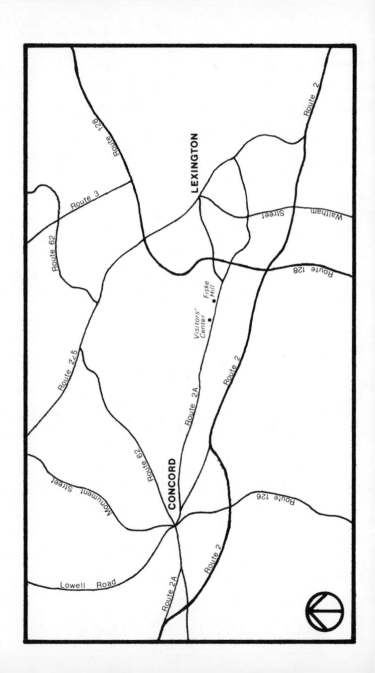

G U I D E :

Where to
Begin a Visit to
Lexington
&
Concord

Visitors to Lexington and Concord will increase the pleasure of their visit by starting it at the Battle Road Visitor Center of the Minute Man National Historical Park. Short film programs orient visitors to the location and relationship of the historic sites the park was established to preserve and interpret. Available here are maps and leaflets for the various historic sites within the park area, but not a part of the park, listing their hours, admission fees, and what they have to offer. Here also are rest rooms and ample parking space, conveniences not always available in or near ancient houses.

The Battle Road Visitor Center is located on Route 2-A in Lexington about half a mile west of Route 128. As Massachusetts Routes 2 and 128 are the major highways nearest to the park, the National Park Service has placed directional signs on both to aid visitors in finding the proper exit. Driving from Boston on Route 2, the visitor should turn on to Route 128 northbound. Almost immediately, by the food-and-fuel service area on the right, appears the exit road for Exit 45-W leading to Route 2-A west, outside the Route 128 perimeter. Park Service signs give fair warning of the entrance to the parking lot for the Visitor Center on the right-hand side of Route 2-A just beyond Fiske Hill, about half a mile from the Route 128 exit.

The Lexington Minuteman

GUIDE TO

Lexington:

Routes for the Tourist

to Follow in Seeing

the Principal Sites

Lexington Green. Visitors wishing to follow the events of April 19, 1775, as they occurred will follow the Battle Road signs from the Visitor Center across Route 128 to Lexington center with its spacious triangular Green. At its point facing toward Boston stands Henry H. Kitson's fine statue, "The Minute Man," erected in 1900. Behind it, at a spot marked by a stone pulpit, once stood the First Parish Church, whose successor now stands beyond the farther edge of the Green. Behind the church was its freestanding belfry, a later version of which is now on the hill on the statue's right hand.

Across the road from the statue, and on its left hand, is

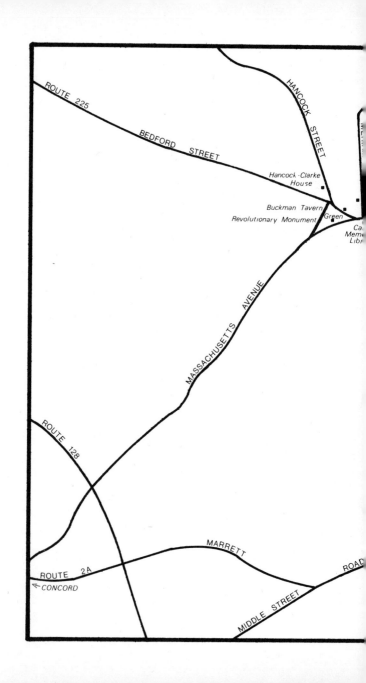

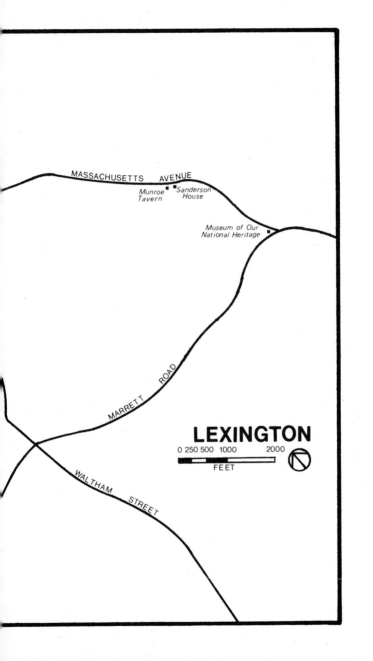

the *Buckman Tavern,* admirably maintained and shown by the Lexington Historical Society, where through the early hours of the morning the minute men had waited. When called together by the alarm, they mustered on the Green at a line near the northeast corner, now marked by a boulder, behind the old church. The stone bears the noble words attributed to Capt. John Parker:

STAND YOUR GROUND. DON'T FIRE UNLESS FIRED UPON, BUT IF THEY MEAN TO HAVE A WAR, LET IT BEGIN HERE!

The British column, seeing the minute men, marched to the right, or Buckman Tavern, side of the church. Major Pitcairn galloped around it to the left. The British volley was delivered at short range, and then the regulars charged with the bayonet. One man, however, was shot as he tried to flee from the church, where he had gone for powder—a strange place for its storage. A Woburn man, captured by the British on their march, was shot as he tried to escape.

A monument to the memory of those who died on Lexington Green was raised in 1799. A blunt obelisk covered with ivy, it stands near the southwest corner of the Green. The Lexington men whose names appear on this *Revolutionary Monument* were first buried in a single lot in the Old Burying Ground beside the present First Parish Church. Their bodies were moved to a tomb behind the monument on April 20, 1835, in ceremonies at which Edward Everett's oration kept his audience spellbound for two hours. Ivy frequently obscures the inscription on the monument, making it hard to read. As it is well worth reading, it is reproduced here.

Sacred to the Liberty & the Rights of mankind!!!
The Freedom & Independence of America.
Sealed & defended with the blood of her sons.

This Monument is erected
By the inhabitants of Lexington,
Under the patronage & at the expense of
The Commonwealth of Massachusetts,
To the memory of their Fellow Citizens,

Ensign *Robert Munroe,* Messrs. *Jonas Parker,*
Samuel Hadley, Jonathan Harrington, junr.,
Isaac Muzzy, Caleb Harrington and *John Brown,*
Of Lexington, & *Asahel Porter* of Woburn,
Who fell on this field, the first Victims to the
Sword of British Tyranny & Oppression,
On the morning of the ever memorable
Nineteenth of April, An. Dom. 1775.
The Die was cast!!!
The Blood of these Martyrs,
In the cause of God & their Country
Was the Cement of the Union of these States, then
Colonies; & gave the spring to the spirit, Firmness
And resolution of their Fellow Citizens.
They rose as one man, to revenge their brethren's
Blood and at the point of the sword, to assert &
Defend their native Rights.
They nobly dar'd to be free!!
The contest was long, bloody & affecting.
Righteous Heaven approved the solemn appeal;
Victory crowned their arms; and
The Peace, Liberty & Independence of the United
States of America, was their Glorious Reward.
Built in the year 1799.

Next door to the Buckman Tavern, and on its right-hand side, is the *Lexington Visitors Center,* operated by the chamber of commerce. It displays a diorama of the battle and dispenses information on what to see and do in town. It also has rest rooms.

Walking from the Visitors Center past Buckman Tavern one passes at the northeast corner of the Green the house of Jonathan Harrington, shot in the fight, who died on its doorstep. (The house is not open to the public.) Swinging right again on Hancock Street, it is a walk of about a quarter of a mile to the *Hancock-Clarke house* on the left side. Here John Hancock and Samuel Adams were sleeping when roused by Paul Revere. The house is now the property of the Lexington Historical Society and contains a fine collection of relics and antiques, the most notable being Major Pitcairn's pistols, captured with his horse during the fighting of the afternoon, when the British had been driven from Concord. Visitors are welcome.

Returning to Lexington Green and to his automobile, the visitor may drive toward Boston on Massachusetts Avenue through the center of Lexington past several more places of historic interest. Just beyond the business district, and on the left-hand side of the road, the Cary Memorial Building stands on a semicircular driveway between the town office building and the police station. The Cary Memorial is an auditorium, with excellent acoustics, used for town meetings, concerts, and other community projects. In its lobby Henry Sandham's famous painting, *The Dawn of Liberty,* presenting his version of the battle on Lexington Green, hangs between the statues of John Hancock and Samuel Adams, whose dedication was a central feature of Lexington's centennial celebration in 1875. Painted in 1886, Sandham's dramatic masterpiece bears little resemblance to Amos Doolittle's engraving based on eyewitness accounts soon after the battle. It belongs to the Lexington Historical Society. Admission to the Cary Memorial at times when the auditorium is not in use may be gained by request to the town clerk in the town office building next door.

A little farther along Massachusetts Avenue, a stone cannon on the left marks the spot where Lord Percy's relief column placed a real cannon to slow down the minute men pursuing the retreating British expeditionary force. One of its balls penetrated the walls of the church on the Green.

About a mile from "The Minute Man" statue, and on the right-hand side of the road, a sign marks the location of the *Munroe Tavern.* Parking space off the road for a few cars is provided. There has been a tavern on this spot since 1695. In 1775 it was owned by William Munroe, a sergeant in the Lexington company of Minute Men, namesake and grandson of the man who began it eighty years before. It is now owned and operated by the Lexington Historical Society.

The house guides are well versed in the history of Munroe Tavern, its additional functions as a store, as the first home of the Hiram Lodge of Freemasons, as host to President Washington in 1789, and as an important stopping place for drovers and farmers bringing food to Boston in wagons and on the hoof, a service which continued until 1850 when the newly completed railroad changed the patterns of travel and put the tavern out of business. In this brief guidebook, however, we are concerned only with the events which took place at the tavern on April 19, 1775.

Lord Percy made the Munroe Tavern his headquarters and a temporary field hospital for wounded men when he brought fresh troops and two cannon from Boston to the rescue of Colonel Smith, Major Pitcairn, and their battered expeditionary force during the retreat from Concord. Theirs was a grim and bloody visit. The bartender, not liking his patrons very much, attempted to run away and was shot to death. A bullet hole in the barroom ceiling remains. The British also set fire to the tavern as they departed, but the fire was promptly extinguished. Relics of the visit of President Washington make pleasanter viewing.

The Sanderson House, next door to the Munroe Tavern, is the headquarters of the Lexington Minute Men, a military body descended from Captain Parker's company, which waited for the British troops on Lexington Green during the early morning hours of April 19, 1775. Historians do not agree on the proper designation of these troops. Were they militia or were they minute men? The records of Lexington's military organizations before the establishment of the republic are not complete. The Lexington Minute Men claim a birth date of December 13, 1773, and that is the date we accept for this guidebook. Founded for the defense of the town of Lexington, this company covered itself with glory on April 19, 1775, served throughout the War of the American Revolution, and has been an outstanding ceremonial unit ever since. The house is now a museum displaying relics of the Lexington Minute Men and of their greatest day. First built in 1689 and remodeled from time to time to meet current needs, the Sanderson house is well worth a visit.

Returning to his automobile, the visitor may continue along Massachusetts Avenue toward Boston until he reaches Marrett Road on his right hand about half a mile from the Munroe Tavern. Turning sharp right on Marrett Road, which is also a part of Route 2-A, he turns right again about a hundred yards from the intersection into the driveway, well marked, leading to the *Scottish Rite Masonic Museum of Our National Heritage.*

As the museum's name implies, the exhibition program emphasizes the growth and development of the United States since its founding; the land and the people on it; the political, social, and economic institutions; heroes and leaders; dramatic events and turning points. The building was completed in 1974. Like most new museums, the permanent collections are small and loan exhibitions are the most frequent occupants of the galleries. "The American War of Independence, 1775–1783," was on view during the summer of 1976. A commemorative exhibition organized by the Map Library and the Department of Manuscripts of the British Library Reference Division, it was one of the best bicentennial shows mounted anywhere. The museum and its library are also intended to be a center for the study of Freemasonry. The parking space is ample. So are the rest rooms.

Upon leaving the Museum of Our National Heritage, the visitor may turn right and follow Route 2-A all the way to Monument Square in Concord. This route picks up the Battle Road, straightened and widened to meet modern traffic requirements, at *Fiske Hill* a few hundred yards east of the Battle Road Visitor Center of the Minute Man National Historical Park.

Visitors wishing a pleasant spot for a picnic along the way from Lexington to Concord, a walk to stretch their legs, and a look at a small historic site, may stop at the National Park Service's Fiske Hill parking space. Picnic tables are scattered under the trees beside it, and a well-marked path makes a broad loop across the shoulder of the hill. Where the path divides, the right-hand way ascends through an open, rocky pasture, enters the woods again, and descends to the site of Lt. Ebenezer Fiske's farmhouse. The path then loops back through the woods close to the Battle Road to the starting point, a total round-trip distance of about one mile.

The foundations of the Fiske farmhouse still stand beside the Battle Road in what is now a quiet meadow. Over its well an engraved stone slab, placed there by the Lexington Historical Society, bears on it one of the more dramatic stories of April 19, 1775. During the British retreat from Concord, James Hayward of the Acton company of Minute Men went to the well for a drink of water. A British soldier emerged from the farmhouse nearby and shouted, "You are a dead man!" Hayward replied, "And so are you!" Both fired their muskets. The soldier fell dead, but his ball, passing through and splintering Hayward's powder horn, opened a dreadful wound in the minute man's side, a wound from which he died in a few hours.

The Fiske farm may also be reached by car along the Battle Road. The rumble of heavy traffic on Route 128 nearby accentuates the tranquillity of the spot.

Less than half a mile west of the Battle Road Visitor Center, a large boulder on the right-hand side of Route 2-A marks the spot near which a British patrol captured Paul Revere on his way to Concord to warn the town that the British were coming. A bronze plaque mounted in the rock tells the story.

Bits of the old road cross the new one from time to time along the way from Fiske Hill to Concord. Visitors who are not afraid to become a little confused may check out the completeness of the National Park Service signs for the Battle Road by following them off Route 2-A where indicated. If all goes well, they will find themselves firmly back on Route 2-A once more at the Bloody Angle in Lincoln, not to lose the route again until they arrive at Monument Square in Concord.

The Bloody Angle earned its name during the British

retreat from Concord. A sharp turn in the road, its high side masked by trees and large boulders, it provided excellent cover for minute men as they fired down upon the approaching British troops. Casualties were heavy.

GUIDE TO

Concord:

Routes for the Tourist

to Follow in Seeing

the Principal Sites

GUIDE TO CONCORD, GENERAL

By the ordinary tourist Concord can be seen (sketchily, that is) in a visit of a few hours. Coming from Boston, a distance of about twenty miles, he can see Lexington and Concord and return in the same day. A longer visit is desirable, however.

As all the important streets in Concord come together at Monument Square, this book uses it as a center from which to visit the sights of the town, and this is the spot to which we have brought the visitor from Lexington. A visitor coming directly to Concord from Boston may follow Route 2 to a traffic signal at the foot of the hill on the Concord-Lincoln town line. Here, at a crossroads, Route 2

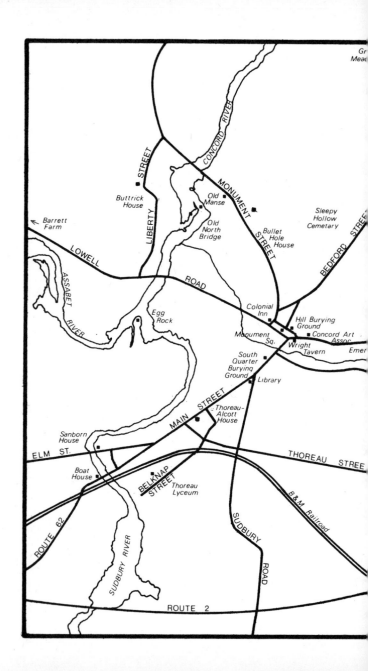

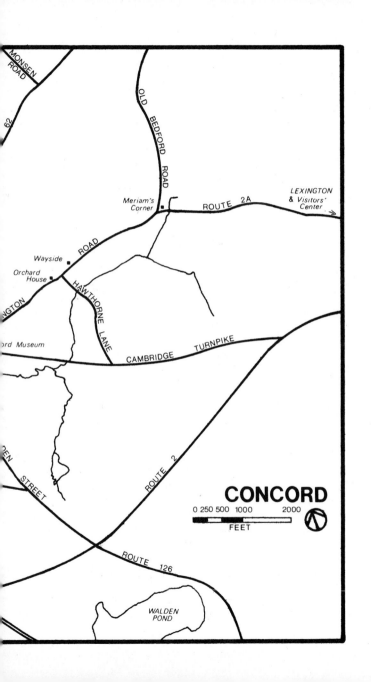

turns sharply left. If the visitor goes straight ahead on the narrow Cambridge Turnpike, following the directional signs for Concord center, he will find himself in a little over a mile at its junction with Lexington Road (Route 2-A), where stands the Concord Museum, home of the Concord Antiquarian Society. A quarter of a mile farther on he will come to Monument Square.

If the visitor will place himself, or imagine himself, at the northerly end of the Square, farthest from the flagpole, he can orient himself. This end of the Square is occupied by the triple building of the Colonial Inn. As he stands with his back to the Inn, at his right Lowell Road leaves the Square, and at his left, Monument Street. In front is the Square proper, which is not square at all, but a grassy oblong. At the end of this a street cuts across the Square: to the right it becomes the Milldam, the beginning of Main Street. To the left it is Bedford Street. Beyond the oblong and the street is the oval containing a flagpole, always considered a part of the Square. Two little traffic triangles stand nearby. Beyond, Lexington Road runs directly away.

The five streets here named will, in this book, be considered one by one. The visitor naturally begins, however, with the Square itself.

THE SQUARE

Here the founders of Concord made their treaty with the Indians, under the great tree whose supposed location is marked, at the entrance to Main Street, by a tablet to "Jethro's Tree" (p. 50). From the Square the Concord company marched in 1689 to Boston to depose Governor Andros (p. 52). Here, many years later, came Paul Revere with messages to the patriot leaders—but not on the historic Nineteenth of April, 1775, for he had been captured by a British patrol in Lincoln. Here in the Square the British, on that day, halted their men, the leaders occupying the Wright Tavern (see pp. 62 ff.) and doubtless hearing from there the volleys of the Fight. In 1786 Job Shattuck and his rioters held the Square for a few hours, in Daniel Shays's unsuccessful "rebellion" (p. 72). And, later, here came and went through many years the persons famous in Concord's literary history—Emerson, Hawthorne, Thoreau, and Bronson Alcott with his daughters.

The Square, then, is a good example of the heart of a New England town, where for more than three hundred years its activities have focused. Here in town meeting were debated and settled the questions vital to the town, with selectman, lawyer, farmer, businessman, and even the humblest inhabitant having his say and his vote. Here, before Concord ceased to be the shire town, were held the county courts on successive days when Concord virtually held a market and a fair until the courts adjourned. Here have been held many of the town's celebrations. And here today Concord gathers for the exercises on Memorial Day, or to sing carols on Christmas Eve.

The Colonial Inn. The Inn, already noted, is made up of three buildings, all of old date. As the visitor faces them, the one to the left once held the store and dwelling of Deacon White, beloved of children for his gifts of sweets, but dreaded by Sunday travelers whom he stopped until the Sabbath was over. The building on the right was once occupied by the Thoreaus while Henry was in college, and here later dwelt his aunts, one of whom, it is said, slipped out at night to pay the tax for which he was arrested (p. 87). The old buildings are now combined into a modern hotel. In the building next to them on Monument Street, John Thoreau, the father, kept store in the 1820s.

On the grass plot in the Square are three war monuments. The one nearest to the Inn was erected to Concord's men dead in the Spanish-American War, the obelisk in the center to the men of the Civil War, the third to those of the First World War.* A monument to Concord's dead in the Second World War, Korea, the

---

*The boulder to the world war dead came from the Nelson farm in Lincoln, and stood in such a position that it may have been used as a cover for Americans firing at the retreating British. But there is no foundation for any story connecting it with a definite person.

The Old Colonial Inn—Deacon White's Corner

Dominican Republic, and Vietnam stands at the turn where Lowell Road joins Main Street at the Milldam not far from the site of "Jethro's Tree."

The buildings around the Square are of no historic note,* except for the Wright Tavern at the farther end. This was built in 1747 and was for many years used as an inn until, in the early nineteenth century, it was turned to private purposes. It now contains shops and business offices. The main part of the building is original.

The Wright Tavern. This is noted for having been the headquarters of the British on the Nineteenth of April 1775, during their brief possession of the town. The officers who occupied the tavern were waited on by the proprietor, Amos Wright. Though he maintained the house for but a single year, his name has clung to it. On the retreat of the companies from the Fight at the North Bridge, there was much confusion in the Square and at the tavern, until after a delay of two hours the troops were at last put in column and started for Boston, only to be attacked at Meriam's Corner and driven under fire from the town. (For more on these events see pp. 62–64, 68–70.)

The Hill Burying Ground. Beside the Roman Catholic Church on the corner of Bedford Street is the Hill Burying Ground, climbing the ridge. (For the ridge see pp. 46, 49, 91.) It is on this slope that Pitcairn and Smith are represented in Doolittle's famous engraving of 1775 as looking over the country while the British regulars parade in the Square below. On top of the ridge, within the cemetery, once stood Concord's first meetinghouse, around which were the earliest gravestones, now weathered away. No stone of any of the town's founders remains. The oldest stone now surviving is Joseph Meriam's. It is dated 1677. As one climbs the path one passes the altar-shaped

*The buildings on the Square are, on the left (looking away from the Colonial Inn), an insurance building, once the courthouse; the Town House; and (across Bedford Street) the Roman Catholic Church. On the right are the brick Masonic Lodge, once a schoolhouse; Monument Hall; and the residence of the Catholic priest, next to which stood the Middlesex Hotel of Emerson's day; and this was most probably the much-disputed site of the house of Peter Bulkeley (p. 26).

monument to William Emerson, grandfather of Ralph Waldo Emerson. (See pp. 18, 38 ff., 61, 67.) Farther up, on the right, are rows of interesting tablets, mostly in the wonderful English slate from which a century and more of New England weather has not effaced the slightest scratch of the stonecutter's tool. Their simple and often quaint designs, and the graceful lines of willow branch or other decoration, relieve the gloom of skull and hourglass, while the epitaphs record the strict virtues and homely achievements of Concord worthies. Here are the graves of Colonel Barrett and Major Buttrick, who commanded at the Fight. (See pp. 25, 26, 54, 65–68.)

Yet, however notable were the excellencies and the social positions of these pillars of the town, their memorials are less celebrated than one erected to a man who was

In the Hill Burying Ground

perhaps the least important of the people of Concord in a day when slavery was still legal in Massachusetts. If the visitor turns left, away from the handsome stones, and crosses a low shoulder of the ridge toward the rear of the nearby church, he will come upon a stone standing by itself, among lilies planted in antislavery days, the stone to John Jack, a slave before the Revolution. In a time when literary feats were more acclaimed than now, this epitaph, written by the Tory Daniel Bliss, was admired as an example of antithesis; it was copied and sometimes translated. Today it can be no less admired, but rather as a summary of a humble life thus skillfully, and even touchingly, rescued from oblivion.*

MONUMENT STREET

Leaving the Hill Burying Ground, walking to the farther end of the Square, and turning to the right, the visitor is on Monument Street. This is the road taken by the British light infantry who on the morning of the Nineteenth of April 1775, marched to occupy the North

*The stone, an old reproduction, has been recut. The inscription reads:

> God wills us free, man wills us slaves.
> I will as God wills, God's will be done.
> Here Lies the body of
> John Jack
A native of Africa who died
March 1773, aged about sixty years.
Tho' born in a land of slavery,
He was born free.
Though he lived in a land of liberty
He lived a slave,
Till by his honest, tho' stolen labors,
He acquired the source of slavery,
Which gave him his freedom,
Tho' not long before
Death the grand tyrant,
Gave him his final emancipation,
And set him on a footing with kings.
Tho' a slave to vice,
He practised those virtues
Without which kings are but slaves.

Bridge and search the Barrett house (pp. 64–65). The American militia had already passed that way, retreating before the greater numbers of the British. The street, even today, has still a semirural aspect. The two houses upon it of particular interest are a half mile from the town.

The House with the Bullet Hole. First of these houses is, on the right and upon a little knoll, the House with the Bullet Hole, the Elisha Jones house, easily identified by its yellow color, its unshingled front, and the old sycamore before it. (The house is not open to the public.) Jones (see pp. 61–62, 70) had quitted the militia to stay with his family. Before the Fight, when regulars came to his well for water, he wisely kept himself out of sight. But as the fleeing redcoats passed the house on their return, he recklessly showed himself in the doorway of the ell. One of the soldiers shot at him: the mark still shows some three feet to the left of the door, under a diamond-shaped pane of glass. Jones's little daughter, from a cellar window, watched the regulars hurry by, some of them limping and bleeding. A portrait of her in old age is at the Concord Museum.

The Old Manse. A few yards beyond the Jones house, on the left, is the gateway to the Old Manse, which stands at the end of an avenue of trees. The house was so named by Hawthorne because until his coming in 1842 it had been occupied by none but ministers, and *manse* is, in Scotland, the name for a minister's house. It was built in 1769 by William Emerson, the patriotic minister. On the morning of April 19, 1775, Emerson retreated from the town with the militia, but, like Jones, went to his own house to stay with his family. He comforted the people of his parish who had taken refuge there, watched the Fight from the height of his own land, and wrote of the American dead, "I saw them fall." At the Manse on that day we must think of the reproachful wife at her window, the frightened women and children outside, and the militant minister eagerly watching the march of the Americans, to make sure that they returned the British fire.

After William Emerson's death while chaplain in the army, his successor, who married the widow and bought the Manse, was Ezra Ripley, for many years minister in Concord when church and town were one. When the people objected to his marrying a woman much older than himself, he declared he would perform no marriages unless his were allowed. They capitulated. In those days every minister was a farmer too, and Ralph Waldo Emerson (Ripley's stepgrandson) describes him getting in his hay when a thunderstorm was coming up. Emerson and the hired man were with him. "He raked very fast, then looked at the cloud, and said, 'We are in the Lord's hand; mind your rake, George! We are in the Lord's hand;' and seemed to say, 'You know me; this field is mine,—Dr. Ripley's— thine own servant!'"

He was a strong Sabbatarian. One Sunday morning, af- ter a heavy fall of snow, his neighbor Buttrick from up the road came with his yoke of oxen breaking out the way to town. To help the minister get to church he turned in at the Manse gate; but Dr. Ripley, from his door, shouted a rebuke for laboring on the Sabbath. Buttrick turned back and went on to town, leaving the pastor to get out of his long driveway as best he might.

Dr. Ripley was a historian of the Fight. When in 1794 the road to the North Bridge was abandoned, he came into possession of it, and loved to tell the story of that famous happening on his own ground. Then, when in 1836 the monument was erected on the nearer side of the river, he gave the land back to the town.

Ralph Waldo Emerson (see pp. 39, 74) was often at the Manse, where he wrote his first book, *Nature,* sitting in the parson's clumsy writing chair, now at the Concord Museum. When Ripley died, Hawthorne next occupied the Manse (p. 88), and after him Ripley's son Samuel, whose wife Sarah was one of the remarkable women of her day, famous for her scholarship when few women studied the classics. A helpmeet to her husband in both home and school, she is said to have tutored a student in Greek while rocking the cradle and shelling peas. A portrait of her is in the Concord Free Public Library.

For another ninety years the Manse came down in the

Ripley family, until in 1939 it became the property of the Trustees of Reservations. This long descent in the same family accounts for the unusual preservation of the Manse in all but its original condition, for only when Samuel Ripley came was any of the older furniture auctioned off, to make room for some of his own. The Manse presents, then, the home through generations of a family of moderate means but high intellect, and hands down to us untouched the picture of earlier times. It speaks in every room and corner of its former occupants and their way of life, displaying in limited space their furniture, their books, their pictures, their simple and even severe daily routine, their active and lofty thought. No one can leave the Manse without a sympathetic understanding of both the men of the Revolution and the generation that produced what Van Wyck Brooks called the "Flowering of New England."

There is not much elbowroom in the Manse. The rooms are small, the stair and hallways narrow. But the furniture is all of that excellent quality which was produced in a small town where the elegancies of the Georgian period were reduced to their structural best. The Saints' Chamber for visiting ministers is spartan, and the lack of conveniences makes the modern man realize the difference between the present and the past, when the well was the source of water, fireplaces gave the only heat, and when in winter steam from the washtubs condensed to frost on the servant's hair.

Mrs. Hawthorne's writings, made with her diamond on the windowpanes, casual records, are charming reminders of her life in the Manse. One such inscription is in the room which both Hawthorne and Emerson used as their study.

The Battleground. Just beyond the Old Manse the road to the Old North Bridge turns sharply left off Monument Street. It is now a footway bordered by double rows of trees first planted by Concord citizens on the sixty-third anniversary of the Fight, April 19, 1838. Until Monument Street was straightened in 1793 and a new bridge built a few hundred yards downstream, the North Bridge gave the only access to the northern part of the town. Visitors may park their cars without charge in the space provided across Monument Street from the entrance to the Battleground. Rest rooms are located at the northern end of the parking lot.

Walking down the footway the visitor first meets, at the bottom of the slope, a granite obelisk dated 1836. Its old-fashioned inscription, stating that here was the "first forcible resistance to British aggression," is an echo of the controversy of 1825 between Concord and Lexington, each striving for the greater glory. Common sense has long agreed that there is honor enough for both.

To the left of the monument, by the wall, is a little space enclosed by posts and chains, with two rough stones and a tablet to the two British soldiers who were buried here after the Fight. The verses on the tablet are by James Russell Lowell. The British Captain Parsons, returning with his regulars from searching the Barrett farm (see pp. 26, 64–65, 70), found the place empty of all but these two, one of whom, in addition to a bullet wound, had received cuts about the head. Rejoining their comrades in the Square, Parsons's men reported what they had seen. The rumor spread that the man had been scalped, and the belief made the regulars more savage on the retreat. The man had not been scalped, however. Tradition tells us that he had been cut on the head by a youth who, coming with a hatchet in his hand from the Manse where he had been chopping wood, found the wounded soldier trying to rise, and in fear or mistaken patriotism had inflicted further wounds.

One sometimes meets the statement that the little space that holds these graves belongs to the British government. This is true only symbolically, in the sense in which Rupert Brooke, English soldier in France in 1914, wrote prophetically of his death the following year:

> If I should die, think only this of me:
> That there's some corner of a foreign field
> That is for ever England. . . .

The land belongs to the town of Concord.

Graves of British Soldiers

Concord Battleground

Set in the face of a massive boulder on the opposite wall is a bronze plaque containing a concise account, about 160 words, of the Concord Fight written by Allen French.

One is now at the Concord River, the current of which is usually sluggish. Hawthorne claimed that he lived beside it for weeks before he learned which way it flowed. The foundation of his boathouse is to be seen upstream from the bridge. From 1793 to 1874 there was no bridge here, and as Emerson wrote in 1836:

> And Time the ruined bridge has swept
> Down the dark stream which seaward creeps.

The present bridge, built by the Department of Public Works of the Commonwealth of Massachusetts, was dedicated on September 29, 1956. It is modeled after the one illustrated in Amos Doolittle's engraving of 1775, but it is stronger and higher. The site of the bridge was changed, after all, because the Concord River's western bank there is so low that it is often flooded. The knoll on which "The Minute Man" statue now stands was built in 1874. Beyond it, to the south and west, the National Park Service has uncovered and resurfaced several ancient roads; one of them, parallel to the river, was followed by Captain Parsons and his redcoats on their way to the Barrett farm. A few yards beyond the bridge another road runs up the hill. By that road the Americans marched down to the Fight.

For the story of the Fight, see pages 66 ff. To understand it here on the ground one needs to remember that after the retreating Americans had crossed the bridge and passed out of sight to await reinforcements, the British occupied the ground. Captain Parsons, with his men, marched to the Barrett farm. Captain Laurie, now in command, posted his companies, one at the fork in the road across the bridge, and two on the hillsides beyond, to protect Parsons's retreat. At the return of the Americans, these companies drew together, crossed the bridge again, and were drawn up in column by Captain Laurie with the intention of maintaining a continuous fire by a method called street firing, usual in the days of single-fire muzzleloading guns. Lieutenant Sutherland and two men crossed the wall into the Manse field to shoot at the provincials. This is clearly shown in the model of the Fight in the diorama of the Concord Museum.* The British volley was probably fired from the very entrance of the bridge when the Americans were about sixty yards away, the effective range of the flintlock smoothbore of those days. Isaac Davis and Abner Hosmer, Acton captain and private, respectively, were killed. On the spot where Davis fell there long grew a bush. " 'Tis the burning bush," wrote Emerson, "where God spake for his people."

On that spot now stands Daniel Chester French's "The Minute Man" statue, typifying the men who took their guns with them to church and field. So this alert figure, leaving his plow, prepares to fight. If this was not already the best-known statue in America, the use of it by the government as a symbol in the Second World War has made it so. On the base is the opening stanza of Emerson's "Concord Hymn," written in 1836 for the dedication of the monument across the bridge.

> By the rude bridge that arched the flood,
>   Their flag to April's breeze unfurled,
> Here once the embattled farmers stood
>   And fired the shot heard round the world.

The lines about the fallen bridge, previously quoted, are from the second stanza of the same hymn. In them Emerson exercised poetic license. Time, in the form of floods, and floating ice and other debris, has indeed swept many bridges from this site, but the bridge which stood here in 1775 was removed by the hand of man.

---

*One sometimes meets the statement that the British fired from the hip. That is easily disproved by any book of tactics of the period. The diorama at the Concord Museum shows the exact disposition: the front rank kneeling, the middle rank stooping, the rear rank erect, and all firing from the shoulder. The model is carefully worked out in every detail. The Doolittle print, however, does not show the British kneeling.

"The Minute Man" statue was made when French was a resident of Concord; he was then but twenty-five years old, and this was his first important work. Referring to his residence and to Emerson's verses, it was said at the time of the dedication that few towns could furnish a poet, a sculptor, and an occasion. At that celebration in 1875, while George William Curtis was the orator of the day, Emerson made a brief address, in the course of which he said, "The thunderbolt falls on an inch of ground, but the light of it fills the horizon."

The Major John Buttrick House and Monument—Liberty Street. Returning from the Battleground to Monument Street and turning away from the village, the visitor crosses the river by the later bridge and, several hundred yards beyond, turns left on to Liberty Street.* On the right he first passes the Major John Buttrick house, a handsome eighteenth-century structure not open to the public. Taking the left road at the fork the visitor will see, in the wall on the left, the sculptured relief to Maj. John Buttrick, who from his own farm led the march to the bridge.

The North Bridge Visitor Center of the Minute Man National Historical Park occupies the large brick house behind the Buttrick bronze figure. It offers the visitor an exhibition room, sales and informational material on the excursion of the king's troops to Concord. A parking lot and rest rooms increase its usefulness. The views from the Buttrick hillside of the North Bridge and the Concord River are beautiful at any season. The old road followed by the Americans to the bridge has been rebuilt as a footway beginning near the Visitor Center.

For many years the only approach to the Battleground entered along the British route from Monument Street,

*Instead of turning on to Liberty Street, the visitor may first follow Monument Street farther, past the Fenn School for younger boys on the right, and then over the shoulder of Punkatasset Hill. Almost at the crest of the road, on the left, is the Hunt farm, where the militia waited for reinforcements before the Fight. Several miles farther on, on the right, is the farm where William Brewster, ornithologist, wrote his journals. He was a different observer from Thoreau, more scientific and less imaginative. The two books published from his journals after his death, *October Farm* and *Concord River,* are of much interest.

bringing the visitor face to face with "The Minute Man" statue. Now the visitor may follow in the American's footsteps from the Buttrick hillside as well.

Following Liberty Street past the Visitor Center, the visitor next sees, on the right, the tablet in the wall marking the field in which the provincials gathered for the attack. In those days the view was not obstructed by trees, and the men could see the smoke rising from the town, prompting Joseph Hosmer to ask the famous question, "Will you let them burn the town down?" (See pp. 61, 66.) It was in this field that the discarded gunflints were found (pp. 65–66). A number of these are to be seen at the Concord Museum.

Proceeding along Liberty Street, one comes to Lowell Road, and can return by it to the town, turning left, or follow it to the right toward the Barrett farm.

LOWELL ROAD AND BARRETT'S MILL ROAD

Lowell Road leaves the Square by Deacon White's corner of the Colonial Inn. Immediately on the left is the Christian Science Church, enlarged from the old dwelling of Deacon Nehemiah Ball, whose disapproval of Thoreau's gentle methods as a teacher caused the latter to whip a few pupils and then resign. A few yards farther on, on the right, is the tablet to commemorate the supposed site of the house of Peter Bulkeley, one of the founders of the town. The road presently traverses a long causeway and crosses the Red Bridge, still so called because it was once wooden and painted red. It is now concrete and steel. From the bridge one can see, to the left, Egg Rock, where the Sudbury and Assabet join to form the Concord River. Just upstream from the bridge is a small parking space and a convenient place to launch a canoe. The area, called the *Old Calf Pasture,* is a delightful picnic spot, on Concord Conservation Land owned by the town. The road swings left just as it is joined by Liberty Street near the spot where Captain Parsons reached it (pp. 21, 64, 70). He came, however, by a road, now partly restored, that skirted the river.

As the visitor follows the curve of Lowell Road to the right, he sees above him, on the right, the picturesque old house (its two parts at an angle) of Edmund Hosmer, friend of Emerson. Proceeding, in half a mile he comes to Hildreth's Corner, where he should note the handsome Hildreth house behind its fence. At this point he takes Barrett's Mill Road, to the left.

In half a mile the road crosses Spencer Brook, on which, on the right, Barrett's Mill once stood. Deacon Thomas Barrett (p. 62) owned this mill in 1775. His son built muskets there during the Revolution. Going on, the visitor passes Strawberry Hill Road as it turns off to the right. The next old house on the right is the Revolutionary farmhouse of Col. James Barrett. It is not open to the public.

On the day of the Fight, Colonel Barrett was very busy on horseback in various parts of the town, until on the hill above the bridge he gave the order to the American troops to march, the order which brought about the Fight. (For him and for the happenings at the house, see pp. 54–55, 64–66.)

Returning to Lowell Road, the visitor may follow it to the left for a mile and a half, when he will see, on the right, the entrance to Middlesex School, a modern preparatory school for boys and girls, whose handsome buildings and grounds are worth an inspection. He will then return to the Square by the way he came.

BEDFORD STREET

Bedford Street, which leaves the Square between the Town House and St. Bernard's Catholic Church, leads, like Lowell Road, Sudbury Road, Lexington Road, and Cambridge Turnpike, to the town for which it is named.

The Alcotts once lived in the house behind the Town House, and there died the third daughter, Elizabeth, whose character is so sweetly, and truly, depicted as Beth in *Little Women.* At the moment of her death, her mother and her sister Louisa, sitting by her side, both believed that they saw a "light mist" ascend from her body and vanish.

Sleepy Hollow Cemetery. At the turn of Bedford Street begins a cemetery whose farther section is known as Sleepy Hollow, a name which was given to it before it was taken into the burying ground. Its peculiar conformation, the flat amphitheater surrounded by steep glacial ridges, had long suggested the feeling of romantic seclusion which gave it the name, possibly taken from Washington Irving's "The Legend of Sleepy Hollow." Hawthorne and his wife liked to linger here. An old road led to the spot on which they planned to build a "castle," where is now his grave. Emerson describes sitting in Sleepy Hollow in October 1837, "to hear the harmless roarings of the sunny South wind." And Hawthorne, in August 1842, found Margaret Fuller there, "meditating or reading." The Hollow was taken into the older cemetery in 1855, Emerson delivering the address, the younger Ellery Channing the poem, and Franklin B. Sanborn writing the hymn.

The Hollow is best entered at the Prichard Gate, two stone pillars on the left hand holding iron gates. One comes within a few yards to a fork in the road; the left-hand road leads, almost at once (on the right), to the Melvin Memorial by Daniel Chester French, erected to three brothers, dead in the Civil War, by a fourth who survived it. The evergreen setting enhances the purity of the marble and the lofty expression of patriotism in the central panel — an emblematic figure which seems to emerge from the stone between the folds of the American flag.*

Returning to the fork in the road, one passes between steep banks into the Hollow itself. The level bottom on the right hand, now covered with graves, was once a cornfield. On the farther side is the famous ridge where lie buried Concord's literary galaxy. The way to it is well marked by engraved stone posts. Following the road as it curves to the left, the visitor comes to the foot of the ridge, and climbing by a winding path straight ahead comes first, on the right

*There is a replica of this central panel in the Metropolitan Museum of Art in New York City.

[28]

near its top, upon the graves of the Thoreau family, the children simply designated by small stones: John, Henry, Helen, Sophia. The Hawthorne family plot is a little farther on to the left of the path. With no other inscription than just the name "HAWTHORNE" on a small low headstone, he lies near other members of his family. The stones in memory of his wife and daughter, Una, tell us that they are buried in London, where they died.

Next, on the right, is the Alcott plot, the children again designated by small stones. Louisa's grave, marked "L. M. A." but also by her full name, is decorated on each Memorial Day because she was a nurse in the Civil War. The father is "A. B. A." (Amos Bronson); the mother is "A. M. A." (Abigail May); Amy is "M. A. N." (Abba May Alcott Nieriker, who actually was buried abroad); Beth is "E. S. A." (Elizabeth Sewall). Meg (Anna Bronson Alcott, who married John Pratt) lies close at hand with her husband.

Farther along on the left is the grave of Mrs. Daniel Lothrop (*née* Harriet Mulford Stone), whose pen name was Margaret Sidney. Her "Five Little Peppers" books have been widely popular.

Across from it the enclosure within chains and massive granite posts contains the graves of Ralph Waldo Emerson and his family. His grave is marked by an irregular, pointed mass of rose quartz, in the face of which is set a small bronze tablet, difficult to read, with his lines expressing so perfectly his feelings about himself:

The passive master lent his hand
To the vast soul which o'er him planned.

(For Emerson see pp. 73–80.) He lies here surrounded by those who meant so much to him in life: his mother; his two wives; his beloved little Waldo,

The hyacinthine boy for whom
Morn well might break and April bloom.

Here also lies Emerson's aunt, Mary Moody Emerson

(p. 74), whose stone bears his characterization of her:

"She gave wise counsels. It was the privilege of certain boys to have this immeasurably high standard indicated to their childhood, a blessing which nothing else in education could supply."

The bronze tablet on Emerson's grave faces the boulder at the bottom of the ridge bearing a tablet to Ephraim Wales Bull, the breeder of the Concord grape. The inscription, "He sowed, others reaped," too well indicates the fate of the man who benefited millions, yet who died in poverty (p. 46). The stone beside it, carved in the form of a tree stump, preserves the memory of his son, Ephraim W. Bull.

Turning back from this point, and following to the right the driveway that leads downward, one comes to the lot of the Hoar family, some of them nationally known. The founder, John (p. 52), is not buried here; the plot holds a later Samuel, "Squire Hoar," and his children. Samuel was a noted and upright lawyer who defended the cause of the slave in South Carolina. Like Deacon White (p. 13) in his day, he prevented Sunday travel past his Main Street home. A Concord farmer, ruefully surveying his grain laid flat by a thunderstorm, was heard to wonder whether, if the storm had come on Sunday, Squire Hoar would have tried to stop it.

His children attained to considerable note. Elizabeth was engaged to Charles Emerson, who died before their marriage; Emerson always regarded her as a sister. Her epitaph, now badly weathered, is well worth reading. Ebenezer Rockwood was attorney general under President Grant. He had a keen and biting wit. George Frisbie was long a United States senator from Massachusetts.

Many other stones in the cemetery are interesting, while as a whole Sleepy Hollow has a peaceful beauty appropriate to its name and purpose.

On leaving Sleepy Hollow visitors wishing to see the *Great Meadows National Wildlife Refuge* will turn left on Bedford Street and drive about a mile to the intersection of Monsen Road on the left. This is not the easiest place to find in Concord. Sharp eyes and a slow approach will help. About half a mile down Monsen Road one arrives at the parking lot for the Refuge. There are rest rooms nearby.

The Great Meadows National Wildlife Refuge extends along the Concord and Sudbury rivers in the towns of Billerica, Carlisle, Bedford, Concord, Lincoln, Wayland, and Sudbury, in two parcels omitting the built-up section of Concord in between. Beginning with the gift by Samuel Hoar of 250 acres of wetland just below the Monument Street Bridge in 1944, it will include about 4,000 acres bordering the rivers when land acquisition is completed. Its importance as a resting and feeding ground for migratory birds increases with the continuing destruction of so many other undeveloped areas to meet the material needs of man. It is a home for many earthbound creatures also, and a joy to naturalists who walk the dike paths which pass through it.

Henry Thoreau knew and loved the Great Meadows and wrote about them often in his journals. So did William Brewster (1851–1919), one of America's finest ornithologists. If Walden Pond is now too overrun by swimmers and picnickers to be acceptable to Henry Thoreau and his disciples, the Great Meadows National Wildlife Refuge would surely delight his soul.

MAIN STREET (THE MILLDAM)

Opposite the beginning of Bedford Street, Main Street leaves the Square. Its first section, with stores on both sides, is called the Milldam. Here, where once probably stood the Indian fishweir ("the Weire at Concord over against the town"), the settlers built for their mill a dam which long held back the millpond with its slight head of water. Into the pond, in 1775, the British rolled the barrels of flour which were afterward salvaged (p. 62). Gradually pond and dam disappeared, though the latest mill building still stands. Where Walden Street leaves Main Street to the left, the stores run with it to Hubbard Street; they also proceed along Main Street nearly to

Sudbury Road. The first of these, opposite Walden Street, a plain and simple brick building with white wooden columns, was the scene of Concord's one and only bank robbery, in 1865. It is now used for business purposes.

Beyond the Middlesex Institution for Savings is the South Quarter, or Main Street, Burying Ground, with many stones as quaint and interesting as those on the hill. It was opened on the other side of the Mill Brook at about the same time as the Hill Burying Ground, according to Concord historian Ruth R. Wheeler, because of an old English superstition against carrying a dead body across running water. The flume at the Milldam was not bridged until 1742. Once the settlement spread across Concord's three rivers, economy and convenience overcame superstition. Buttricks, Barretts, Hosmers, and others were carried without incident from their outlying homes across the rivers to both cemeteries, with no ill effects, so far as we know.

The Public Library. In the fork of the road, where Sudbury Road goes to the left, stands the Concord Free Public Library, which contained in 1975 some 175,000 volumes, about 30,000 of which are housed in the Loring N. Fowler Memorial Library, the West Concord branch. The total circulation figures for 1975 of books and phonograph records at both libraries reached 280,130, a large figure for a town whose population was then about 17,000, according to the 1975 town census.

The Concord Alcove contains only books written in Concord or by Concord authors. Emerson and Thoreau are so well represented as to have their own alcoves containing books by or about them. Manuscripts by Emerson, Thoreau, Hawthorne, the Alcotts, Mrs. Lothrop, and other lesser-known Concord authors are carefully preserved and occasionally exhibited.

The central octagon room displays French's fine statue of Emerson; it shows him in the favorite dressing gown in which he used to write. In addition, there are busts of Thoreau, Bronson and Louisa Alcott, Hawthorne, and other distinguished Concordians—Samuel Hoar; Ephraim

Wales Bull; Ebenezer Rockwood Hoar; and the donor of the library, William Munroe, among them.

The white-paneled trustees' room contains the table used in the White House by presidents from Madison to Grant. Three small dioramas by Louise Stimson depicting Concord as it was in the mid-nineteenth century are set in the left wall of the corridor leading from the octagon to the children's room. A small gallery over the front hall provides a pleasant and well used place for changing exhibitions.

The Concord Academy. Leaving the Library and proceeding west along Main Street, one passes various former dwellings of the Thoreau family. Most of the houses on the right, or river, side of the street are now occupied by the Concord Academy for girls and boys, founded in 1922.

The Thoreau-Alcott House. On the other side of the street, the third building from Belknap Street is the Thoreau-Alcott house. (The house is not open to the public.) Here the Thoreau family lived for a number of years, and in the room to the right of the front door Thoreau died. To the left of the house, and stretching from the rear, once stood the family pencil factory. This is the latest of the Thoreau houses, several of which probably had a little factory close by.

When the Alcotts, on the wave of Louisa's prosperity, bought the house, Alcott added, on the right, the wing to hold his library, prominent in which were the many volumes of his journals. These are now in the Houghton Library of Harvard University but are still privately owned and controlled.

If the visitor follows Main Street still farther to the fork and takes the right branch, *Elm Street,* he will see, on the right, just as he reaches the bridge over the Sudbury River, the brick-end house built by *Franklin B. Sanborn,* friend of the famous writers. In this house he gave shelter to the poet William Ellery Channing, the younger. Sanborn is best known in Concord for an incident in 1859, when he lived on Sudbury Road. United States marshals attempted to arrest him for his connection with John Brown; he resisted;

the town turned out to help him; Judge Hoar hastily produced a writ of *habeas corpus*; and the marshals were forced to depart, to molest him no more.

From this point, taking River Street opposite the Sanborn house, the visitor comes to Main Street again, and, turning right, crosses the South Bridge, once occupied by British troops (p. 64). The *South Bridge Boat House* is the only public boat livery on the Concord, Sudbury, and Assabet rivers above Billerica. Thoreau knew and loved these rivers. His journals have much to say about them. They have changed very little in appearance since his time, especially through the marshy areas now a part of the Great Meadows National Wildlife Refuge. A day on them in a hired canoe with a picnic lunch is a most rewarding experience, whether one cares about Henry Thoreau or not.

Following Main Street as it swings left under the railroad bridge, the visitor first finds on his right the home of Joseph Hosmer (pp. 61, 66) and close beyond it the *Hosmer Cottage* of the Alcotts, now somewhat changed. This house is said to be described as the "Dovecote" in which Meg of *Little Women* began her married life. Neither is open to the public.

Returning on Main Street toward the Milldam, turning to the right on the second street, Thoreau Street, the visitor is, from this point, on the most direct route to Walden Pond, for the street, running almost straight, joins Walden Street on its way from the Milldam to the pond. But if he leaves Thoreau Street at the first right-hand turn, proceeds on to Belknap Street, and crosses the railroad, he will find, farther on the right, numbered 156, *The Thoreau Lyceum.*

Long ago, before Texas struck oil, this section of Concord was called Texas, mostly by people who did not live in it. Now both Texas and Concord have changed, and the designation Texas for this part of Concord has been forgotten. Next door to The Thoreau Lyceum once stood the first house owned in Concord by the Thoreau family. Referred to by the Thoreaus as the Texas house, it was built by Henry and his father with their own hands in 1844–45. Their pencil business was conducted in an attached lean-to shed constructed of lumber salvaged from the shanties of the Irish laborers who had built the Fitchburg Railroad and then moved on.

The Thoreau Lyceum is owned and operated by the Thoreau Foundation, a small, nonprofit, public organization formed in 1966 by Concordians who believed that there should be a Thoreau center in the town where he was born and lived most of his life. It contains and displays Thoreau memorabilia and changing exhibitions based on his varied interests. There is a small research library and a gift- and bookshop. Behind it stands a replica of the Walden house. Visitors are welcome. There is a small admission fee. This is the best place in Concord to obtain up-to-date information on conditions at Walden Pond, a wise precaution before attempting a visit, as the following paragraphs will make clear.

WALDEN POND

W alden is blue at one time and green at another, even from the same point of view," Henry David Thoreau wrote in *Walden.* "Lying between the earth and the heavens, it partakes of the color of both."

Returning to Thoreau Street from The Thoreau Lyceum, the visitor should turn right and drive south toward Walden Pond. On the way, at the foot of Brister's Hill, Walden Street comes in from the left just before the entrance to the Hapgood Wright Town Forest. Across the street the Concord-Carlisle Regional High School, with its landscaped grounds and parking lots, fills the slope of Brister's Hill.

Walden Street continues across Route 2 through the Walden Pond State Reservation, now operated by the Massachusetts Department of Environmental Management's Division of Forests and Parks. Parking is permitted only in two off-street parking lots for which a fee is charged, this fee including also the right to use a table and fireplace for two hours, the bathhouse, and the bathing beach. Parking on Walden Street from the intersection of Brister's Hill Road to the Lincoln town line and beyond is prohibited.

Walden Pond is one of the nearest and most convenient public bathing beaches to the city of Boston. One and a half million people used it during the year 1975, according to official estimates. Very few of them knew or cared anything about Henry David Thoreau. Those who do are advised to make their visits when the weather is too cold for swimming.

As one faces the pond from Walden Street, the stone posts marking the site of Thoreau's Walden house are on the right-hand, or northern, side of the pond about halfway to the tracks of the Fitchburg Division of the Boston & Maine Railroad on the western end. From his house Thoreau could watch the passage of the steam cars, "their train of clouds stretching far behind and rising higher and higher, going to heaven while the cars are going to Boston." The site is reached from the entrance of the reservation by a rough wood road or by the path along the shore beginning at the bathhouse. There are a few stone directional signs along the wood road.

The exact location of Thoreau's house at Walden has long been a matter of controversy. It was moved away and the chimney taken down shortly after he vacated it. The cairn erected by admirers on its supposed site was not begun until 1872 when all traces of the building had disappeared. Depending on the memory of friends, a spot was chosen as the probable position of the hut. But, since it did not tally with Thoreau's minute description of it in *Walden,* it has always raised questions. Other spots have been pointed out as more probable, and even marked with corner posts, but not until 1945 did anyone have the curiosity and perseverance to solve the problem.

Roland Wells Robbins of Lincoln had the practical idea of searching the sandy hillside for the foundation of the chimney. After many weeks of probing and digging, he finally unearthed the unmistakable evidence he needed. In his book, *Discovery at Walden,* available at The Thoreau

Lyceum, he tells the fascinating story step by step. The hearth had been removed and the accumulation of a century had obscured the traces on the surface, but the solid masonry of the foundation was exposed, untouched since Thoreau built it with his own hands. Later, three corner posts and a center post of the house, and four corners of the woodshed were found, as well as many other proofs which are incontrovertible.

The words written by Thoreau at Walden and afterward have been heard as far as the shot fired at the North Bridge, and their meaning has been interpreted in as many different ways. We will let him explain in his own words, drawn from *Walden*, why he went there.

When I wrote the following pages, or rather the bulk of them, I lived alone, in the woods, a mile from any neighbor, in a house which I had built myself, on the shore of Walden Pond, in Concord, Massachusetts, and earned my living by the labor of my hands only. I lived there two years and two months. . . .

In any weather, at any hour of the day or night, I have been anxious to improve the nick of time, and notch it on my stick too; to stand on the meeting of two eternities, the past and future, which is precisely the present moment; to toe that line. You will pardon some obscurities, for there are more secrets in my trade than in most men's, and yet not voluntarily kept, but inseparable from its very nature. I would gladly tell all that I know about it, and never paint "No Admittance" on my gate. . . .

My purpose in going to Walden Pond was not to live cheaply nor to live dearly there, but to transact some private business with the fewest obstacles; to be hindered from accomplishing which for want of a little common sense, a little enterprise and business talent, appeared not so sad as foolish. . . .

I left the woods for as good a reason as I went there. Perhaps it seemed to me that I had several more lives to live, and could not spend any more time for that one. . . .

Truly, Thoreau traveled a good deal in Concord.

Returning all the way on Walden Street, the visitor comes to the Milldam and the Square.

LEXINGTON ROAD

Lexington Road leads out of the Square past the *Wright Tavern* (p. 15), next to which stands the *First Parish Church* (formerly Meetinghouse). Although the tablet in front of this speaks of the First Provincial Congress as meeting here, it refers to the building burned in 1900. In that structure, which was standing in 1775, the Congress indeed met, with John Hancock and Samuel Adams as leaders, and with William Emerson (p. 16) as chaplain. In the vestry Thoreau made his dramatic and stirring "Plea for Captain John Brown," which changed the hearts and opinions of many of his townsmen. The present structure was built in 1901, much like its predecessor, but of somewhat different proportions.

Opposite is a row of houses, some of which are interesting for their age and style, being pre-Revolutionary. In one is the *Concord Art Association,* which holds a permanent collection, and frequent loan exhibitions. In the brick-end house of later date lived Thomas Whitney Surette, a modern leader in music education. Still farther along, the house next to the corner is the house of *Reuben Brown,* harness maker and Revolutionary patriot, whose brief entrance into and exit from history was on the day of the Fight (p. 60). The house was set on fire, but extinguished, on that day. The building, little changed from its original structure, is of the farmhouse type, built around a great central chimney, with a small entrance hall and a winding stair. It is now a private home, not open to the public.

The house at the bend of the road, the Heywood house, is likewise Revolutionary. Its picket fence, now gone, went back to Emerson's day, and the late owner used to relate the following. Emerson's wife would not allow her husband to smoke either in the house or in the village. He used,

The Unitarian Church

therefore, to light his cigar at his door on going to the village, but would conceal it behind one of the pickets of this fence. Whenever he perceived this, young Heywood would slip up to the fence, and if the cigar were still alight, would enjoy a few puffs himself. More he did not risk, for Emerson, returning, would retrieve the cigar, light it, and finish it on the way home.

The Emerson House. Turning the corner toward the left, one sees ahead on the right (at the fork where the Cambridge Turnpike leaves Lexington Road) the square white Emerson house under its pines. Here from 1835 till his death in 1882 Emerson exemplified his "plain living and high thinking" (pp. 74, 77-78). With a patient kindness which rose from his belief that he could learn something from anyone, he allowed many cranks and oddities to break in upon his time. But here also he received many famous people, including most of the literary celebrities of his day. Thoreau, handyman and close friend, lived here with the family at different periods. Emerson worked in the room to the right of the front door. Though the contents of this study, even to the shutters, have been taken to the Concord Museum across the road, the room has been fitted again with his belongings; the parlor has been untouched. The house is open to the public daily except Sundays from April through October.

To the left of the house, beyond the orchard, once stood the arbor intended as a summer study for Emerson. Designed by Alcott in his favorite style, of crooked branches of trees, it was not finished without the aid of Thoreau. When it was completed, Mrs. Emerson dubbed it the "Ruin," which it was in but a few years. Nor was it ever put to its intended use, being too drafty and full of mosquitoes.

The Concord Museum. Across the Turnpike from the Emerson house, in the fork of the two roads, stands the museum of the Concord Antiquarian Society, on Emerson land given by the family. The house, its collection, and its arrangement, are noteworthy. The furniture was gathered about a century ago by a poor man, in a time when taste was

Victorian and earlier pieces could be picked up for little or nothing. Taken over by the Society and housed for many years in the Reuben Brown house, in 1930 the collection was put in the present fireproof building. Besides the furniture, surprisingly complete in wood, glass, china, and brass, and of all periods, there is good wainscot from old demolished houses. The whole is assembled with correctness and taste in a series of period rooms, from the provincial to the early Victorian. In them the visitor can follow the development of styles in chairs, beds, bureaus, and other furnishings; he can see similar advances in utensils and in the fireplaces; while the wainscot, from crudest to finest, also shows the improvement in household art to the McIntire period and the beginning of the decline about 1840.

Often called the best small collection of American antiques, the museum is rather a display of the development of a New England town of but moderate wealth. The cabinetwork of the craftsmen who served Concord, simplified from the more elegant productions of the seaboard, shows a dignity and charm that is far from crudity. The lover of antiques in general will enjoy the collection as a whole, while the student of styles will find genuine examples on which to base his theories.

Apart from this purely cultural interest, the house holds reminders of Concord's history. The Society owns the one remaining of the two Paul Revere lanterns; various weapons used at the North Bridge; and some of the gunflints of the minute men, discarded when they changed them in preparation for the Fight. It has also, in a diorama or model of the Fight, a dramatic representation of it. It has the clumsy old chair in which Emerson wrote *Nature* (p. 75). There are also Emerson and Thoreau rooms. The former contains, in a room built to the exact dimensions, the furnishings of Emerson's study—the pictures, the rocker in which he used to write with his portfolio on his knee, and the calendar with the leaves torn off to the month of his death. The Thoreau room, intentionally small, bare, and simple, contains much of the furniture of his hut at

Walden (pp. 36–37, 86), portraits, and books. (For the diorama, see footnote to p. 65.)

Thus the little museum sets forth, in very large part, the social, martial, and literary history of Concord. It is open to the public for a fee most of the year.

A special feature is the courtyard of the house, closed by the ancient exterior of the oldest wing, and made picturesque by the lilac from the Thoreau farm on the Virginia Road. Here too is the most charming of herb gardens, quite in the old style, much studied and imitated by modern gardeners.

Orchard House. Leaving the Museum grounds on the opposite side from the Emerson house, the visitor proceeds along Lexington Road until he finds on the left (about three hundred yards), slightly set back behind a widening of the road, and within its own fence, the large and comfortable Orchard House, long the home of the Alcotts (1858–77), and the one most closely associated with their fame (pp. 80 ff.). The land was once the site of the home of John Hoar and his workshop for Christian Indians in 1675; probably the old frame is a part of the present Alcott house (p. 52). In this a large part of *Little Women* was written. The great elm in front, which long loaned picturesqueness to the grounds, is now gone, with most of the old apple trees that stood on the left, in which the children played. But the house is very much as it used to be when Louisa humorously called it "Apple Slump."

It is more visited than any other house in Concord. Here the fictional characters of *Little Women* come again to life, and by the aid of the furnishings of each room, and the costumes in the cases, seem to reenact the scenes of the book. Yet here too is Alcott life as described in our later pages, with much self-denial and hardship, serenely borne by the philosopher, and more bravely, if sometimes grimly, by his wife and daughters. Art is present in the drawings by May Alcott (Amy) on the walls, fortunately preserved down to the present. Here is a splendid record of family life maintained on a high plane, and handing down to later times the lesson of love and perseverance.

Hawthorne's Wayside

The School of Philosophy. To the left of the house stands the bare building of the summer School of Philosophy, the darling of Alcott's later years (1879–88), not without a little ridicule from his gifted daughter. It was much attended, during its brief life, by the lessening group of transcendentalists, whose earnest discussions failed to produce any notable results.

Wayside. The next house, while it was Alcott's Hillside and afterward Hawthorne's Wayside, has a still earlier interest as the home of Samuel Whitney, Revolutionary patriot, who here housed some of the military stores before the British came. The building has some structural reminders of that early period. Alcott, coming in 1845, found the house, according to Hawthorne, "a mean-looking affair, with two peaked gables. . . . He added a porch in front and a central peak, and a piazza at each end. . . . Mr. Alcott expended a good deal of taste and some money (to no great purpose) in forming the hillside behind into terraces, and building arbors and summer-houses of rough stones and branches of trees, on a system of his own." Alcott was a devotee of what he called the Sylvan style. Fortunately none of his creations survives (p. 40), though his terraces remain. Up these terraces the Alcott children used to plod in their childish play of *Pilgrim's Progress,* dropping their burdens at the top, like Christian in the story. In the house Hawthorne himself made extensive changes, the most noticeable of which, built for his second period in the house, is the so-called tower. This is a three-story addition, the top floor of which provided a study in which he could have the seclusion which was essential to him. It contains the standing desk at which he liked to write.

Because of his many years abroad (pp. 88–90) Hawthorne occupied the house only in 1852–53 and 1860–64. Yet as the only house he ever owned he took in it particular satisfaction, and when he began his life in it he wrote, "I felt myself, for the first time in my life, at home."

The house has been well preserved, largely through the care of Mrs. Daniel Lothrop (Margaret Sidney) (pp. 29, 91). Her husband, a Boston publisher, bought it as a summer home for his family, and Mrs. Lothrop occupied it at intervals until her death in 1924. Here she wrote many of her books, the *Five Little Peppers and How They Grew* and others. The Wayside is now owned and operated by the National Park Service.

The house and its furnishings present mementos of its literary inhabitants, of whom more have dwelt or made long visits here than in any other house in Concord. In his first period at the Wayside Hawthorne wrote his *Tanglewood Tales* and the biography of Franklin Pierce; but his second period was not successfully productive, in spite of all his efforts.

In the barn adjoining the house the Alcott children held some of their youthful plays. On the wooded ridge behind the buildings Hawthorne used to sit in meditation, or walk up and down. Here, in his *Septimius Felton*, he laid the scene of his hero's duel with the British officer. And here he had his interview with the youthful William Dean Howells, after which he introduced him to Emerson with the statement that he found the young man "worthy." The

Grapevine Cottage

spot was unfortunately sadly devastated by the hurricane of 1938.

Grapevine Cottage. Two doors down, on the same side of the street, is the *Grapevine Cottage,* where in 1849 Ephraim Wales Bull produced the Concord grape. It is not open to the public. A goldbeater with a taste for horticulture, he came to Concord in 1836, and devoted himself more to his hobby than to his trade. Discovering that the best grapes of his day often were spoiled by early frosts, he tried to breed an early and hardy variety. Beginning with a wild grape, he crossed it with others, until eventually, after years of experimentation, he found a seedling which satisfied him. This he named the Concord. Its commercial success was enormous, but others profited instead of Bull, which embittered him. At one time he was in the legislature, which he served usefully in agricultural matters. At that time he dressed elegantly, so much so that Emerson once, at a distance, mistook him for Alcott. His son said that it was Bull. "Oh, well, Bull," said Emerson. "That is quite another matter. I thought Alcott looked more like a gentleman and less like a philosopher than usual." But when Bull retired he laid aside his top hat and wig, let his own white hair and beard grow long, and loved to putter among his plants in his dressing gown and silk skullcap. He grew older, feebler, and poorer, and finally died (1895) in Concord's Home for the Aged. Trusting no one in business after his reverses, he never would put on the market four other grapes which, out of some twenty-two thousand seedlings brought to maturity, he considered equal to the Concord. His tombstone says truly that he sowed, but others reaped (p. 30).

Meriam's Corner. A half mile farther along Lexington Road, one comes to Meriam's Corner, where the Old Bedford Road comes in from the left. A tablet in the wall records the event which happened here, when the British quitted Concord (p. 70). The head of the column of grenadiers reached the corner, to the left of which was the Meriam homestead, still standing. At the same time the light infantry flankers marched down from the ridge, and the minute men of Reading and Billerica approached on the Old Bedford Road. The British joined, and marched across a little bridge then existing on the road to Lexington, where now is but a culvert. The regulars marched "with very slow, but steady step, without music, or a word spoken that could be heard. Silence reigned on both sides." After crossing the bridge the rear guard turned and fired, though by one account the Americans fired when the bridge was full. Next, as the firing became general, appeared the men from the North Bridge, coming around the ridge. Wrote one of them, "a grait many Lay dead and the Road was bloody."

Here began the running fight which drove the British all the way back to Boston (p. 70).

Thoreau's Birthplace. From Meriam's Corner the Thoreau lover will go on to the Thoreau birthplace. Following the Old Bedford Road to the left of the Meriam house, and taking Virginia Road, the first road to the right, he will pass on the left, about a third of a mile from the turnoff, the original site of the Thoreau house. Here now stands a later house, sometimes marked with the sign, "Thoreau Farm." The original house was moved many years ago to its present position, the next beyond the newer house, on the same side of the road. A private house, it is not open to the public.

Retracing his steps, the visitor returns to the village, and may revisit anything that has specially interested him. There are many more places to be seen in Concord than those listed in this Guide, and more is to be learned of its events and people. These can be followed up, at least in part, in the History which follows, and more completely by the aid of the Bibliography at the end of the book, which will provide much reading matter concerning a town which, for its size, is one of the most interesting in the United States.

HISTORY:

A Brief Study
of the First Two
Hundred and Fifty
Years
1635–1885

THE COLONIAL PERIOD

Concord's history divides itself naturally into three periods: the founding, with the early struggles to survive; the Revolutionary, with the reason for and the facts of the Concord Fight; and the literary, with the local story of some of the country's greatest writers. These follow each other in order of time but in the same scene, for Emerson walked where his ancestor Bulkeley made the treaty with the Indians, and Hawthorne dwelt but two hundred yards from the North Bridge. It is worth noting that through the whole story the geography of the town connects itself with the events of its history.

Topography. Where a little stream, centuries ago, ran

straight through level land, the Indians made a fishweir to trap the spring run of shad and herring. On broad meadows, farther away, they cultivated, here and there, patches of maize. On two rivers which joined and made one they paddled their canoes, and along the banks they hunted waterfowl. A certain ridge which entered their territory from the east, and twice turned till it ran northerly, probably was of no use to them. So too with the three hills which rose from the plain, unless their woods could be hunted for game. At one spot the Indians held their feasts of river clams, and the shells remain to tell of it. At others the savages made and abandoned and made again their cobbled fireplaces. If the region was the scene of Indian warfare, there is no record of it. But where they hunted they lost their arrowheads, and where they worked they left their mortars and pestles, axes and awls. They still occupied the area in 1635, and to this day the soil renders up the stone tools that tell of them.

The Founding. When white men came they saw that the brook, if dammed, would run a mill. The rivers were unimportant: they led to the wrong place by the sea.* But the meadows they liked, especially those spots where Indian hoes and clearance fires had prepared the way for better cultivation. (The English had yet to learn that the rivers would overflow the lower spots.) And the ridge would be of use, for it would hold their meetinghouse and their homes in a place suited for defense. So they bargained for a six-mile square, and built the church and dam and dwellings, poor houses, half dugouts in the hillside. Their first road began at a spot, at the first rise of the ridge, where many years later would begin the running fight with the retreating British. Following on below the ridge, the road passed the place where one day would be bred the Concord

---

*The rivers are the Sudbury and the Assabet, which at Egg Rock meet and form the Concord, which empties into the Merrimack. Though never useful for navigation, they were formerly a great means of recreation, as proved by George Bartlett's guidebook of 1885; he addressed his book, not merely to Concord pleasure seekers, but also to tourists coming by water from farther away.

grape, and others where yet would dwell the Alcotts, Hawthorne, and Emerson. The road turned a corner, and running straight for awhile, passed the future sites of the best pre-Revolutionary houses, of the church of the original parish, and of the Town House in what is now the Square. Again the road turned, and seeking a site to cross the river, found one that was used for many years, where the British met their first defeat. All this is still the main artery and the heart of modern Concord. It is true that other important places in Concord lie farther away, also that many changes have occurred. The millpond is gone, and the millbrook is all but hidden. But the old dam, now a busy street, is still called the Milldam; and the simple geography of plain and brook and ridge still influence the daily ways of man.

The first man to map the region was William Wood, who did it crudely in his book of 1634. Probably the first to examine the place with an eye to settling was Simon Willard, "Kentish souldier," who came to the colony in the same year. A fur trader, he doubtless learned of the place from the Indians, and led here the group of "planters." Chief among these were the ministers, Peter Bulkeley and John Jones, both "silenced" in England for their Puritanism. Their families, and those that accompanied them, amounted to perhaps sixty-five in all. The founders bore names long known in Concord history: Hosmer, Buttrick, Hunt, Ball, Meriam, Flint, and still others. Their grant from the General Court was dated September 12, 1635.

An equally necessary step was the treaty with the Indians. Tradition says that it took place under a great tree, the site of which is still marked on the Square. The white men "on the one party, and Squaw Sachem, Tahattawan, Nimrod, Indians, on the other party," came to an agreement. The white men gave tools, knives, cloth, and shirts, and fitted out the medicine man, husband to the female sachem, with "a suit of cotton cloth, an hat, a white linen band, shoes, stockings, and a great coat." Then "Mr. Simon Willard, pointing to the four quarters of the world, declared that they had bought three miles from that place,

east, west, north, and south; and the said Indians man-
ifested their free consent thereunto."

It was this free consent of the Indians, some have said,
that gave the name of Concord to the town. Others,
however, have believed that the name, first mentioned in
the Boston grant, signified the perfect agreement among
the settlers themselves. At any rate, in the summer of 1636
their crops were planted on the meadows, and their first
crude houses were completed, not far from the equally
simple church which stood on the ridge above the present
Square.

Life in Concord during its first years was hard.
Bulkeley had brought money with him, and established
various members of the town on farms, cutting down his
own resources. But the soil was harsh and the trees many;
wolves ate the swine; the meadows flooded; and most of the
settlers were unskilled in the new life. They "cut their
bread very thin for a long season," said their historian.
"Thus this poore people populate this howling Desart."
They felt their isolation, being the only ones away from
tidewater, miles from the nearest whites, and fearful of the
savages. At length some of them, led by the minister Jones,
went away to Connecticut, leaving Bulkeley and the
remainder more lonely still. It was only after another few
years that Concord began to prosper.

King Philip's War. Fear of the Indians, freely admitted
by the settlers, was not justified in these earliest times. The
tribesmen of that generation helped the settlers, bringing
them game, and teaching them how to plant the Indian
corn—with a few herring, caught in the spring run, in
every hill as fertilizer. It was not until 1675 that the fear of
Indians was justified. Then Metacomet, "King Philip," led
the Indians against the whites. One raid came too near the
town, when the two brothers Shepard, working their farm
in what is now Littleton, were ambushed and slain, and
their sister Mary carried off. She escaped, however, and
came to Concord with the alarm. Concord men were in the
famous fight at Brookfield, where various of them were
killed, and where Capt. Thomas Wheeler was brought out

of the skirmish by his son Thomas, both of them wounded. The party, besieged in a house, was at length rescued by men under Simon Willard, then in his old age.

Concord village was spared an attack by the reputation of its pastor, Edward Bulkeley, for when the Indians consulted whether the town should be raided, a chief declared, "We no prosper, if we go to Concord. The Great Spirit love that people—they have a great man there—he great pray!"

Two incidents during this war give honor, if not to Concord, at least to one of its citizens. Among the Indians there were converts to Christianity, who remained peaceful while their tribe went to war. Yet they were under strong suspicion by the whites; therefore to keep them from either doing or receiving harm they were brought together in Concord by John Hoar, who housed them and built them a workshop on his own land, where now stands the Orchard House of the Alcotts. Feeling against them ran high, however; Hoar's humanity and protection were thought not to be enough. The Indians were taken from him by the forceful intervention of soldiers and herded together on an island in Boston Harbor, where they suffered much hardship till the end of the war.

Hoar's spirit was better appreciated, however, when a new need arose. The Indians raided Lancaster, and carried away Mrs. Rowlandson, the wife of the minister. It was believed that she could be ransomed; yet no one dared to go among the Indians with the money until Hoar offered to go. He went, was received with hatred and threats, yet his steady courage brought success, and he returned with the woman.

The peace which followed King Philip's War was presently disturbed by the coming of *Governor Andros,* who expressed doubt as to the citizens' titles to their land. To satisfy him were made the depositions as to Concord's bargain with the Indians from which we have already quoted. Yet to the protests of various towns Andros declared that he valued an Indian's mark upon their treaties no more than the scratch of a bear's claw. Chiefly for this the colony rose against him, seizing the opportunity offered by the news that in England William of Orange had landed to expel King James. In this little revolt Concord took its share, on the first of the town's three historic Nineteenths of April. On that day, in 1689, Concord's company was mustered in the Square, and marched to Boston to take its part in the imprisonment of Andros.

In England, William was successful; yet he brought to an end one period of Massachusetts history. Believing the colony to be too independent, he changed its form of government. From a colony it became a province, with stricter supervision from the mother country. Under the new charter Massachusetts flourished; there were other wars, but more distant. And Concord was peaceful and prosperous until there loomed the struggle against England itself.

THE REVOLUTIONARY PERIOD

Preparations. The Stamp Act of 1765 made no outward disturbance in Concord, but by it the minds of the townspeople must have been prepared for further trouble. For the tea controversy, on the question of taxation, brought from the town in 1774 the declaration, characteristic of the times, that while the people would risk their fortunes and lives in defense of the king, they would equally risk them in defense of their charter rights. But the king's authority and the people's liberties proved to be deeply opposed. The town entered wholeheartedly into the struggle against new laws; its meetinghouse held the earliest sittings of the First Provincial Congress; and when the province began to gather munitions for an army, Concord became the most important storehouse for those means of war. Cannon and their carriages, powder, bullets, camp kettles, and other necessaries were assembled in the town. The Massachusetts leaders believed that in such a patriotic place these stores could be safely kept; and it was for this reason that Concord, and Lexington on the road to

Concord, saw the opening scenes of the Revolutionary War.

Perhaps because of its responsibility for the stores, Concord was earlier than most towns in organizing the minute men. These were the younger and more active men from among the old organization of the militia of the province; the two companies were enrolled in January 1775. There were two militia companies as well, with the Alarm Company, composed of old men and boys; but the minute men were pledged to be ready at a minute's warning. So literally did they take this promise that they carried their guns with them to church and to the field.

The minute men companies of the neighboring towns were organized into a regiment of which John Buttrick of Concord was major. Similarly the militia companies were formed into a regiment of which James Barrett of Concord was colonel. Barrett, the older man, had retired from military duties; but he was recalled. Slow and unwieldy on foot, he was still able to ride his horse, as he proved when occasion demanded.

Through the winter the companies of all the neighboring towns drilled at home and met occasionally in musters. A British officer sent out by General Gage, the British governor in Boston, reported these "trainings" with much ridicule, little thinking that he himself would someday retreat before the homespuns.

Every act of either side drew both parties toward war. The governor and his troops were practically cooped up in Boston. Each practice march that the soldiers made into the country was jealously watched, lest one should be made in earnest. Nothing that Gage did could long be kept a secret from the Boston patriots. Nor could the actions of the provincials be kept entirely secret from the governor. He knew that stores were being assembled in Concord, and that an army was being formed against him. It was only common sense for him to destroy the stores if he could, to make the army helpless. Realizing this, the Committee of Safety, when it held in April its sessions in Concord, required Colonel Barrett to keep men and teams ready, by day or night, on the shortest notice to remove the stores. Then, as if knowing that the emergency was at hand, on the eighteenth the committee ordered the removal of many of the stores to towns farther away. And that very night the work began, although no warning had come that in Boston the British expedition was on the move.

For General Gage had at last made up his mind to act. A good administrator, his patience and tact had been great; but he had lost various chances to seize the Massachusetts leaders, and even now he merely tried to take or destroy the stores. He had made no effort to lay hands on Dr. Joseph Warren, openly living in Boston, and the most active man there in watching and blocking the British moves. The mechanics and craftsmen in Boston spied narrowly on all that was done, and brought the news to Warren. And their reports on the night of the "eighteenth of April, in seventy-five," were that troops were on the move, assembling at the foot of the Common, not far from which it was already known that the rowboats of the men-of-war had been moored in waiting. Warren sent for two messengers, both of whom were experienced in riding post for the Committee of Safety.

One of these was William Dawes, whom Warren instructed to attempt to leave Boston by the only land exit, to Roxbury. But as soldiers held the Neck, and Dawes might not be allowed to go out on a night when some movement was in progress, Warren also sent for Paul Revere.

Revere was silversmith and engraver, craftsman extraordinary, and also a patriotic messenger on various occasions. He had lately been to Concord with a message from Warren, and on that occasion had prepared for this very emergency. To Concord, of course, both he and Dawes were sent: it could be the only objective of a secret expedition of the troops. With instructions from Warren, Revere put his plan into execution. Against British orders, he had a hidden boat; but lest he fail in his attempt to leave the town, he sent a friend to signal patriots in Charlestown, across the river, that the troops were leaving Boston by boat. The signal was two lanterns hung in the steeple of the North Church. One of those lanterns is now to be seen in Concord, at the Concord Museum.

Revere succeeded in crossing; though there was light from a young moon, he was not seen by warships or British patrols, and on the Charlestown shore he found friends awaiting him. On Deacon Larkin's horse he rode away on his errand. He took the most direct route, toward Cambridge; but blocked by British mounted officers, whom he saw in the moonlight, he turned back, gave them the slip, and galloped to Medford. From there, and as far as Lexington, he roused every important household on the route.

LEXINGTON

Until three days before, the Provincial Congress had been sitting at Concord, with its two chief members, John Hancock and Samuel Adams, directing every move. On the night of the eighteenth the two were sleeping at the house of the Reverend Jonas Clarke, in Lexington, with a guard of minute men outside. When Revere arrived, about midnight, the sergeant asked Revere to make no noise. "Noise!" he rejoined. "You'll have noise enough before long. The regulars are coming out!"

The town was immediately roused. Hancock and Adams rose and dressed; but while Hancock wished to stay and fight, his wiser companion tried to persuade him to go away. The minute man company assembled, and under its captain, John Parker, mustered on the Green. Then there was a long waiting. Dawes arrived, and he and Revere set out for Concord, accompanied by young Dr. Samuel Prescott, a Concord man who fortunately happened to be courting his sweetheart in Lexington that night. For when the three met suddenly a second patrol of British officers, Revere was taken and held, Dawes turned back toward Boston, and Prescott alone, escaping by jumping his horse over a wall, roused the captain of the Lincoln minute men, and himself brought the news to Concord.

The Lexington company, mustered on the Green in a night that was moderately cold, received no news from the scouts that they sent down the Boston road. At length their captain dismissed them to houses nearby, and to the Buckman Tavern, almost on the Green, to assemble instantly on the first summons.

Dawn began to break, a chilly morning, when Revere appeared again. His captors, recognizing him, had questioned him, and he had bluffed them with the story that the whole country was in arms and ready for the approaching expedition, of which, to their surprise, he appeared to have accurate news. To warn the expected column, these officers hurried to the Boston road, releasing all their prisoners. Revere hastened back to Lexington and told his story to Hancock and Adams, who quickened their departure. Revere followed them with a trunk of Hancock's papers, which he took to a place of safety. Returning once more, he was just in time to observe what happened on the Green.

The detachment which Gage sent out from Boston numbered probably about seven hundred men, consisting of the grenadier and light infantry companies of all the regiments in Boston. They were therefore unaccustomed to acting together, and not used to their superior officers. These were Lt. Col. Francis Smith of the Tenth Regiment, and Maj. John Pitcairn of the marines. Pitcairn was a steady and sensible officer, not unpopular even with the patriots of Boston. But Smith was heavy, dull, and slow, good for routine duties, but unfitted for an expedition requiring enterprise and initiative.

Blunder after blunder caused delay after delay. The troops mustered late in the evening, but it was some time before they were in their boats, of which there were not enough. Two trips were required to ferry them across the Back Bay and to Lechmere Point in Cambridge. Then there was a long wait for their rations, some of which the men threw away as the food grew heavy on the march. Wet to the knees, the men at length began their journey from the marshes; then they went fast. In the very early morning they passed through the outskirts of Cambridge and through Menotomy, now Arlington. Various stories are told of incidents on the way, but nothing happened to stop the troops until they neared Lexington. They met the scouts who had been sent from Lexington for news. But the British advance patrol, marching silently on the sides of the road, made prisoners of them, and the troops marched on. The light infantry were in the lead, under command of Major Pitcairn.

Now came to warn them the mounted officers who had earlier captured Revere. Pitcairn, halting his troops and consulting, also received the statement that an American had attempted to fire at Lieutenant Sutherland, scouting in front. The major therefore ordered the troops to prime and load, and to march on, "but on no account to Fire, or even attempt it without orders." And so the troops moved forward, entered the village of Lexington, and approached the Green.

Meanwhile the Americans had received their final alarm. Thaddeus Bowman, scouting to find why no further news of the British had come, was warned by his skittish horse, which shied at the advance picket of the British, and enabled him to see, beyond them, the head of the marching column. Galloping back, he brought the news to the Lexington captain. The drum was beat, and the minute men came running to the Green. Their sergeant formed them in two lines. There were perhaps eighty of them, drawn up in full view of the Concord road, by which the British were expected to pass. It was sunrise, and long shadows fell across the Green.

Perhaps then Parker uttered the words credited to him: "Stand your ground; don't fire unless fired upon; but if they mean to have a war, let it begin here!" Strong words, and suited to a desperate situation; but here was one in which the minute men, parading without defense, invited annihilation from a force many times their number. Months of inaction had fretted the regulars; they were exasperated by the provocations given by the Yankees. If the Lexington men, drawn up where they had a right to be, had expected the troops to pass by on their mission, they were mistaken. The head of the column swerved, entered the Green, and marched directly toward them.

The Lexington church stood then on the Green, on the corner nearest Boston. The column passed on one side; and Pitcairn, seeing what was happening, spurred his horse around the other, to take a position where he could command both the troops and the militia. Various mounted officers were with him.

And Parker saw the unwelcome necessity of the situation. His men could not stand against so many. He gave the order "to disperse and not to fire." Slowly and unwillingly his men began to break ranks.

What happened then is not, and probably never will be, clear. Eyewitnesses on both sides disagree: each said the other fired first. The evidence cannot be reconciled. No doubt Pitcairn uttered the words long imputed to him: "Disperse, ye rebels! Lay down your arms and disperse!" But he solemnly asserted that he ordered his own men not to fire, and tried to prevent it.

But his men were eager for the prey so helpless before them. Paul Revere, just then coming within sight of the Green, declared that the first shot fired was from a pistol. Others said the same. Now, in all likelihood the only pistols there were in the hands of the mounted officers, and some were young and hotheaded. However it happened, a shot was fired, then others, and then the advance company fired their guns and rushed in with their bayonets.

Some Americans fell dead on the spot. Others, mortally wounded, dragged themselves away—like Jonathan Harrington, who reached his own doorstep to die at his wife's feet. And still others, fiercely resisting, were bayoneted where they stood—like Jonas Parker, killed while trying to reload.

For the Americans returned the fire, from the Green and from the tavern. In the excitement and the smoke they did but little damage: Pitcairn's horse was hurt, and one of the regulars. But the British possessed the ground, and drove from it the remaining minute men. Eight of the Americans were killed, ten wounded.

The troops, if unrestrained, might have broken into the tavern, the church, and the nearby houses, bayoneting all that they found. But Pitcairn and his officers, and Smith who now arrived, quieted the men. They were formed again, admonished, and ordered to the road. It could not have been half an hour before they were gone, and the men and women of Lexington flocked to the scene, to take up the dead and to care for the wounded.

The townsmen were not cowed. The British had cheered before they marched away. But they would have to come back by that very road, and the men of Lexington prepared for a second encounter, when they could take vengeance for their losses (pp. 70–71).

CONCORD

Of all that had happened Concord knew nothing. Young Dr. Prescott had arrived long before dawn, with Revere's tidings. Longfellow was wrong when he wrote in his poem that Revere "came to the bridge in Concord town." Only Prescott's warning came to the town; and so the men in authority, wishing like those in Lexington to learn whether anything was really going to happen, while they still kept on with the hiding of stores, sent a man to Lexington to bring back news.

This was Reuben Brown, harness maker, whose house still stands on Lexington Road. Mounted, he rode to Lexington to find what might be happening. And he arrived at the Green just when the rattle of the British guns rang out, and when smoke enveloped the scene. Bullets whistled; perhaps one came near Brown; and he might have seen the head of the column of grenadiers, advancing on the Boston road. Brown thought he had seen enough, and turned and galloped back.

But Major Buttrick was not satisfied. He asked if the British had fired with ball. Brown's answer is quaintly delicious. "I do not know, but think it probable." Buttrick doubtless drew his conclusions; yet action proceeded on the assumption that the militia must not fire first.

The Reuben Brown House in 1915

As time passed and still the British did not appear, the minute man companies were sent down Lexington Road to reconnoiter. They had reached the end of the ridge, at Meriam's Corner, when across the level ground they saw the British column descending the opposite slope. The regulars were so superior in force that the minute men marched back and reported to the field officers, waiting with the militia on the ridge opposite the meetinghouse. It was wise to depart and wait for reinforcements. The little force, consisting of the Concord and Lincoln companies, marched to another height overlooking the road to the North Bridge; here Joseph Hosmer was appointed adjutant and the whole put in order. The minister, William Emerson, urged that the place be held: "Let us stand our ground; if we die, let us die here." But wiser counsels prevailed: the provincials were too few. As the British were seen again, marching toward the bridge, the Americans once more retreated before them.

Two men quitted their posts in the line, leaving the ranks as they passed their own houses, to stay with their families and defend them. One was Elisha Jones: his house is now known as the House with the Bullet Hole. The other man was the minister himself, going to the Manse, where were not only his family, but also the wives and children of some of his parishioners. Jones kept himself out of sight. His house contained a number of barrels of beef, with salt fish and other stores, but it was not entered. Neither were the Manse grounds, where the minister, ignoring his wife's entreaties to come indoors, remained outside with his people, watching what happened at the bridge and on the roads.

On their arrival the British had taken possession of the center of the town. Smith and Pitcairn made their headquarters at the Wright Tavern, and they sent out parties to search for munitions. Two large brass cannon, twenty-four pounders, were discovered at the Jones Tavern. The exulting British spiked them and knocked off their trunnions. With the same feeling, the troops cut down the Liberty pole, which was on the ridge. Bullets were found and thrown into the millpond, and barrels of flour were also rolled into the water. But later the Americans dragged out both bullets and barrels, when it was found that the barrels had swelled, and only the outer part of the flour had been damaged. No powder was found, nor many of the important stores, for the Yankees turned aside the search of the British by one pretense or another.

Thus in Timothy Wheeler's barn were stored many barrels of flour belonging to the province, together with others of his own. He readily admitted the British searching party and showed the barrels. "This," he said, pointing to his own property, "is my own. I am a miller, sir. Yonder stands my mill. This is my wheat; this is my rye; this is mine."

"Well," said the officer, "we do not injure private property." And he withdrew with his men.

The officers, therefore, were humane, and their men under control. Some of the soldiers, trying to get information from old Deacon Thomas Barrett, threatened him with death as a rebel. He remonstrated mildly: they might save themselves the trouble, for he would soon die of himself.

The Wright Tavern

"Well, old daddy," they replied, "you may go in peace," and they released him.

Yet there was plenty of excitement in the town. One woman, as if to receive company, put on one fresh apron after another until she was wearing seven. Her neighbor, wiser, rescued from the church the Communion silver and put it in the soft-soap barrel in the Wright Tavern. When taken out next day, it was pot-black.

The excitement grew when cannon carriages which had been found were burned near the Town House. Martha Moulton, "widow-woman," went to the tavern and begged Pitcairn to extinguish the fire. The officers said good-naturedly, "O, mother, we won't do you any harm. Don't be concerned, mother." But she persisted, and they sent and extinguished the fire which threatened the building.

It is the more difficult, therefore, to ascribe to Pitcairn ("a good man in a bad cause," wrote the patriot Ezra Stiles) the story that at the tavern he stirred his toddy with his finger, and boasted that thus he would stir the Yankee blood that day. Smith, well known as the opposite kind of man, was dull enough not to see the situation that he had put himself in. More than to anyone else, the story belongs to him.

In spite of all care, a fire was started in Reuben Brown's harness shop. It was soon put out. More deliberate was the burning in the Square. The smoke of these fires was seen by the militia beyond the town, and led to action, as we shall see.

Some detachments of the regulars were sent farther away. One company was sent to the South Bridge, and preventing passage there, searched houses in the neighborhood. A second detachment was sent to the North Bridge. The British knew that some two miles beyond the bridge was the home of Colonel Barrett, where many supplies had been stored. Six companies of light infantry, under Captain Parsons, were therefore sent on a search. Leaving half of them at the bridge to secure his retreat, Parsons went on with the rest. He did not particularly notice that, as he approached, a man was seen plowing in a field—the only man seen peacefully occupied that day. Nor did any of the British guess that cannon were lying in a furrow, and the man was plowing earth over them.

At the house the search produced no great results. Much had been carried away or concealed. Open barrels in the attic, topped with feathers, hid bullets, flints, and even cartridges; but the soldiers did not suspect. More cannon wheels were found, however. When it was proposed to burn them on the spot, and Mrs. Barrett remonstrated for the sake of the barn, they were burned in the road. She refused to take money for food, saying, "We are commanded to feed our enemies." When officers threw the money in her unwilling lap she said, "This is the price of blood." And when she refused liquor to the men the officers sustained her, saying that they had killed men at Lexington, and more bloody work was sure to follow.

Meanwhile Captain Laurie, in command of the companies at the bridge, posted them across it, one at the bridgehead and two on the hillsides beyond, to watch and prevent any movement by the Americans. These had retreated to Punkatasset Hill, a mile farther away, where slowly reinforcements came in—the Bedford and Acton companies, the smaller one from little Carlisle, nearby, and then singly or in groups from Chelmsford, Westford, and Littleton. Concord men returning from hiding the supplies joined their companies. And as the force grew in numbers, and anxiety for the town increased, they marched down again to a spot overlooking the bridge, where for a time the British below watched them with interest and suspicion.

Hosmer put the companies in line, the minute men on the right, the militia on the left. Barrett, who had been very busy all the morning on horseback, was now on the ground, with Buttrick and the selectmen. It used to be said that the men were ordered to discard all doubtful gunflints,* to make sure of an effective fire. This tale was proved true only a few years ago, when nearly a hundred gunflints were

*A gunflint (the flint of a flintlock, used to strike fire, the only method of those days) was square, entirely different from an Indian arrowhead. Flint of this quality is not native stone.

found in the field, an unusual number that can only have come from the one cause.

As the men looked in the direction of the town, they saw smoke rising from it in new and greater quantities. It looked as if the town were on fire. And Hosmer, alarmed and indignant, went at once to the group of older men. Breaking into their consultation, he pointed to the smoke and asked the question, now historic, "Will you let them burn the town down?"

The decision was immediate: to march into the town, or die in its defense. Colonel Barrett gave the order for the troops to march. But on no account were they to fire first.

The two British companies on the hillsides below saw that the provincials were too strong for them, and marched back to join the third one at the bridge. Lieutenant Sutherland, whom we have seen near Lexington, had come with the British as a volunteer. Impatient for something to happen, he was just starting for the Barrett farm; but thinking that "it would be disgracefull to be taken by such Rascals," he too went to the bridge. Here Laurie waited long enough to perceive that his own position was not safe. Therefore he marched his three companies across the bridge; then strangely, quite forgetful of Parsons two miles away, he ordered men out upon the bridge to take up the planks. Sutherland, eager to be of use, undertook to supervise the work.

On roads recently restored by the National Park Service the Americans marched down the hill, then turning a corner, marched directly at the bridge. Buttrick was leading, and by his side, as aide, marched Lieutenant Colonel Robinson of Westford. First in line behind them came the Acton company, whose captain, Isaac Davis, had said as he accepted the post, "I haven't a man that's afraid to go." The Concord minute man companies followed, and then the remaining minute men and militia, even down to the Concord Alarm Company of old men and half-grown boys. They marched two-and-two, perhaps four hundred in all, and their fifes played the stirring tune of the "White Cockade."

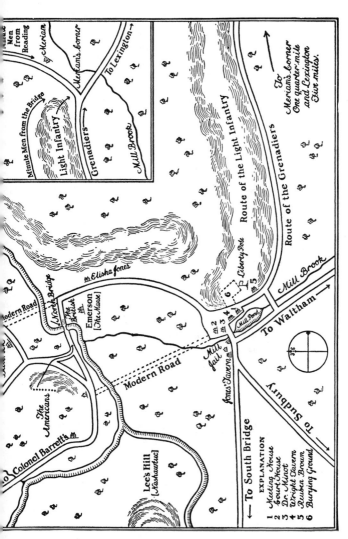

Map of Concord Fight

As they approached the bridge, Buttrick shouted to the soldiers taking up the planks, ordering them to "desist." They quitted the spot just as Laurie, to make his fire more effective, ordered men into the fields to right and left of the bridge, ready to fire on the advancing Americans. Only one officer obeyed the order: Sutherland, who took two men with him into the Manse field.

Above and behind him, the minister, Emerson, stood at the height of his own land, anxiously watching everything that happened.

In warning, next, the British fired a few shots into the river, and then another directly at the Americans. The ball passed under Robinson's arm and wounded an Acton and a Concord man. The Americans marched steadily on. Buttrick cannot have been far from the bridge, with the Acton men close behind, when the front ranks of the regulars fired their volley. It killed the Acton captain and one of his men, and wounded others in the ranks. One man, cut by a bullet, cried out that the British were firing jackknives.

Buttrick, leaping into the air as he turned to his men, shouted, "Fire, fellow-soldiers, for God's sake, fire!" The word was passed; the front ranks fired; and men behind them broke from the ranks to fire at the British. Then all surged forward to take the bridge.

A few more British shots may have been fired, but in haste, and harmless. And the regulars broke. Four of their officers, out of eight, were wounded, among them Sutherland in the field. A sergeant was hit; two men were killed; another was mortally wounded; and several were hurt. The remainder (there were but a hundred and twenty men at most) saw Buttrick and the Acton men already on the bridge. And so they ran, carrying with them their officers and the few veterans who would have held them. In that minute or two the Concord Fight was over.

This was Concord's share in beginning the Revolution—attack, no longer defense. It was heroic. These men knew the law: no people could have studied the situation better. They knew the penalty of rebellion, of failure. They

The Old Elisha Jones House — The House with the Bullet Hole

had every reason to fear trained soldiers better armed than themselves. But protecting their homes, and at last defying their king, they struck to make themselves free.

There was one further incident. As the straggling British passed the house of Elisha Jones, its owner rashly showed himself in the doorway of the ell, his gun in his hand. Some regular with gun still loaded, angry and glad of the mark, fired at him. The shot went wide—its hole is still to be seen, about three feet to the left of where Jones stood. The soldiers passed on, and Jones wisely put himself out of sight. But the bullet hole remains to tell the story.

Like most militia, the Americans were disorganized by their success. Some took up their dead and wounded; others, rallied and marching forward, saw a reinforcement of grenadiers approaching from the village, and took post behind walls. Forgetful of Parsons, still beyond the bridge, Smith, who led the grenadiers, halted and marched them back. The provincials also forgot, and Parsons led his men in safety to the village. The Fight had happened a little before ten o'clock. It was not until about noon that Smith, wasting valuable time as he tended his wounded, marched for Boston. Equally wasteful of their time, the Americans watched and waited for any movement that Smith might make. They did not block the roads, but were merely ready to fight again. Sudbury and Framingham men came to the ground, and all were prepared to strike the British.

Smith made a good disposition as he left the town. His wounded were in commandeered chaises on the road, guarded by the grenadiers. To right and left, on the meadows and the ridge, the light infantry flanked the little column. (On the ridge, readers of Hawthorne may recall, the writer set the scene of the duel between the British officer and Septimius Felton.) A mile from town the British reached Meriam's Corner again (pp. 46–47). And there began the famous running fight. All the way to Lexington the militia, fighting without order, every man for himself, took post behind any shelter (sometimes, forgetting the British flankers, too close) and fired at the retreating regulars, giving them no time to form, and no object at

Amos Doolittle's Engravings

of the Battle of

Concord and Lexington

P L A T E I

The Battle of

Lexington

April 19, 1775

1. Major Pitcarin, at the head of the Regular Grenadiers.
2. The Party, who first fired on the Provincials at Lexington.
3. Part of the Provincial Company of Lexington.

Presented by Felix Channing May

gular Companies on the road to Concord?
e Metinghouse at Lexington.
he Public Inn.

A. Doolittle Sculpt

The four hand-colored engravings by Amos Doolittle of the Battles of Lexington and Concord were published in New Haven, Connecticut, on December 13, 1775. A charter member of the Connecticut Second Regiment of Guards, Doolittle arrived in Cambridge with his regiment on April 29 and soon thereafter visited the battle scenes. Tradition tells us that he was accompanied by the itinerant painter Ralph Earl, who made sketches based on the testimony of eyewitnesses. From these sketches Earl made paintings, and from these paintings Doolittle engraved his four plates.

P L A T E II

A View

of the

Town of Concord

Plate II. *A View of the*

1 *Companies of the Regulars marching into Con*

2 *Companies of Regulars drawn up in order*

3 *A Detachment destroying the Provincials.*

Colonel Smith & Major Pitcairn viewing the Provincials
who were mustering on an East Hill in Concord.

A. Doolittle Sculp!

[The] Townhouse. [The] Meetinghouse.

A painting of plate II, *A View of the Town of Concord,* hangs in the Concord Museum. Scholars do not know whether it is the work of Ralph Earl or a later copy by an unknown artist of the Doolittle engraving. No paintings of the other three plates are known.

P L A T E III

The Engagement at

the North Bridge

in Concord

Plate III. *The Engagement*

1 The Detachment of the Regulars who fired f
on the Provincials at the Bridge

North Bridge in Concord.

The Provincials headed by Colonel Robinson &
Major Buttrick. 3 The Bridge

A. Doolittle Sculp.

The four engravings provide excellent illustrations to *A Narrative of the Excursion and Ravages of the King's Troops, under the Command of General Gage, on the Nineteenth of April, 1775: Together with the Depositions Taken by Order of Congress to Support the Truth of It.* Isaiah Thomas published this *Narrative* in Worcester in May. An early copy of the *Narrative* was sent to London on board the schooner *Quero* from Salem on April 28. Delivered on May 28 to the Lord Mayor of London, a man not sympathetic to the royal government, it was circulated rapidly all over England. General Gage's official account arrived two weeks later, too late to diminish the impact of the American version.

PLATE IV

A View of

the South Part

of Lexington

Plate IV. A View of the

1. Colonel Smith's Brigade retreating before the Provin[cials]
2. Earl Piercy's Brigade meeting them.
3 & 4. Earl Piercy & Col. Smith. 5. Provincials.

Part of Lexington

N. Doolittle. Sculp.

The Flanckguard of Percys Brigade.
Fieldpiece pointed at the Lexington Metinghouse.
Burning of the Houses in Lexington.

If the Battles of Lexington and Concord were not military victories for either side, the reporting of them was clearly a propaganda victory for the Americans. Time has since transformed propaganda into tradition. More than two hundred years after the event, it is safe to say that we will never know in precise detail what actually happened. There were, after all, no impartial observers on the scene. If this Guide strays from sober history from time to time, it does so in the direction of tradition.

The Doolittle engravings are here copied with permission from the reproduction made by the Meriden Gravure Company for Goodspeed's Book Shop, Inc., from the original owned by The Connecticut Historical Society.

which to charge. As the British approached Lexington, the men of that town were ready and took their revenge.

Yet there the regulars, tired and with empty guns, met safety. Smith's one wise action of the day was in the early morning, when he sent to Gage to ask support. And now in Lexington Lord Percy's brigade came to save him, having with it two fieldpieces which awed the militia more than all the muskets. Under this protection the fugitives rested awhile; then the two detachments marched back to Boston. They were harried all the way by more and more provincials; they lost both men and pride; but they gave as well as took, for many Americans, venturing too close, learned that the redcoats still could strike. And the regulars made good their retreat. Late in the day the wearied remainder reached Charlestown in safety, and were ferried across the Charles (which Revere had crossed by the light of the moon) to the rest and comfort of their barracks. But that very night the Americans closed in around Boston, and began the siege which after eleven months, under Washington, drove the British from the town.

Only four Concord men (three of them captains) were wounded on that day. Concord soldiers took part in the siege of Boston. Since Cambridge was occupied by the American troops, Harvard College removed to Concord, and remained through an academic year. Classes were held in the meetinghouse, and in private houses. College Lane, a little-used highway at the western end of the town, is today the only reminder of that episode. Yet three members of the class which graduated here returned to stay: Jonathan Fay, lawyer in the town for thirty-three years; Dr. Hurd, who practiced here for fifty-five years; and Ezra Ripley, for sixty-three years minister (p. 19).

In the disturbed period after the Revolution, Concord was once more the scene of rebellious activity, this time largely by old soldiers against the very government which they had defended. Great public burdens, high taxes, business depression, bad money, and imprisonment for debt of men who had served the country were the grievances. In September 1786, Job Shattuck and two to three hundred men, as a part of the now almost forgotten "rebellion" of Daniel Shays, took possession of Concord Square, closed the courthouse, forbade the courts to sit, and petitioned for redress. The little uprising, which ended in dispersion of the shabby muster, nevertheless had a good influence in hastening Massachusetts's acceptance of the new Federal Constitution.

The Concord Fight was the town's one direct experience of war, yet Concord men have always been ready to serve. As the Fight occurred just eighty-six years to a day after the town's militia marched out against Andros, so after another eighty-six years, on another Nineteenth of April, Concord's company marched to the Civil War. They have fought in all wars since. The four monuments on the Square, and the beautiful Melvin Memorial in Sleepy Hollow, testify to the devotion of Concord men.

The North Bridge

Concord

in

Literature

By a curious chance, Concord's literary story is linked with its earlier fame. William Emerson, the fiery minister, acted as chaplain in the Revolution, and died of camp fever. His son, also William, lived as minister in Boston, but died almost equally young. Meanwhile Ezra Ripley, successor to the first William, married the widow, and lived in the Manse. He was helpful to his step-grandchildren, sometimes housed the family, and said once to Ralph Waldo Emerson, "I wish you and your brothers to come to this house as you have always done. You will not like to be excluded; I shall not like to be neglected." It was this influence which made Emerson so much of a Concordian. In the town where his ancestors had lived (for he was a descendant of three of Concord's ministers) he himself came to dwell. And it was Emerson's influence which brought the Alcotts here, to some extent Hawthorne as well, and helped to develop the genius of Thoreau, a native of the town. Others, such as Margaret Fuller, Channing the poet, George William Curtis, came and went; but these—living, writing, dying, and buried in Concord—were Concord's literary group.

EMERSON

Ralph Waldo Emerson, born in Boston in 1803, was often in Concord in his youth, but did not come here to live until 1834. Meanwhile he had been a minister, but resigned his work because he could no longer follow the old forms. He had struggled with ill health; he had married, but was a widower. He and his mother first boarded at the Manse. His brother Charles was also in the town, where lived likewise his eccentric aunt, Mary Moody Emerson, she who, born in 1774, used to boast that she was "in arms" at the Concord Fight, and whose oddities did much to conceal her strong good sense and high ambition for her nephews. Emerson wrote for her tombstone, "She gave high counsels." And he lived up to them. Coming to Concord to live, he wrote: "Hail to the quiet fields of my fathers. . . . Henceforth I design not to utter any speech, poem or book that is not entirely and peculiarly my work." He never swerved from that plan. Writing in the field of religion, morals, and social ethics, where thousands had worked before him, he struck out a new line of thought which helped to mold his generation and which influences America to this day.

In 1835 Emerson married Miss Lydia Jackson of Plymouth (whose name he changed to Lidian for the sake of euphony), and bought for his residence the house at the beginning of the Cambridge Turnpike. Here his children were born; and here he lived for nearly fifty years, until his death in 1882. His habits were simple. Daily when at home he walked in the fields or woods, and returned to write down in his study his thoughts or observations. These he would work over until they suited him, and then, following the custom of that day when so much of America's thinking was expressed from the lecture platform, he would set forth on his tours, delivering in towns and cities the lectures which he later published as his essays.

Emerson's one systematic book is *Nature,* his earliest. It has structural form; the thought can be outlined from beginning to end. The book was published in 1836. But no other was so written according to plan. The remainder of his many volumes contain his essays, each written to a title and around a central subject which it illumines rather than dissects. The reader does not finish one and rise with the complete knowledge of Emerson's thought upon it, whether it be "History," "Self-Reliance," "Spiritual Laws," "Prudence," "Heroism," or "Friendship" (to take some of the titles in the First Series of his *Essays*). Instead the reader rises inspired with thoughts aroused by the essay, and with his own conduct attuned to following them. Few essays did more to strengthen the young men of the day than the second of these, "Self-Reliance," with the ancient injunction, "Know Thyself," fortified by the advice, "Trust Thyself."

The lecture system of those days was aided by the innumerable Lyceums which, originating in New England, spread all over the country to towns of any size. In the Lyceums, forerunners of the Chautauqua, Emerson lectured for many years, meeting the hardships naturally inherent in the stagecoaches, the crude sleeping cars, the badly heated hotels of mid-nineteenth-century America. Famous from his beginning, yet under suspicion because of his almost revolutionary thought, he made his way to complete acceptance, until his words were household in all forward-looking families in a period of controversy when new ideas were resisted by the old, welcomed by the young. Emerson was the prophet of youth when in the spiritual war against slavery the nation was coming to take sides, when the radicalism of intellectual Europe was assuming its own form on American shores, and when the old theology was crumbling, partly under his blows.

He first shocked the Puritan world, long entrenched, self-satisfied, and crystallized into a dead formalism, by his Harvard Divinity School Address in 1838. Men of the old school at once protested at thoughts disturbingly new; it was many years before that center of conservatism invited him again. Yet invited again he was, after a long battle in which the odds turned to his side. Emerson welcomed the new science, so disturbing to the old theology. He advocated new social ideas, now fundamental and instinctive with all America. His method was not to attack the old, but to state the new, and to let his ideas stand or fall by themselves, without defense or rejoinder by him. And so sure was he of his ground, so telling in the simple force of his principles, that opponents were silenced, and support grew. Long before his death he was the venerated prophet of the new America.

One does not dissect and explain Emerson's philosophy as one can explain the structure of some other system of thought. For Emerson's ideas can never be so formulated: they are rather a way of life, never dry, always inspiring thought and action.

Some of his most memorable writing is in his poems, which cover a wide range of technical performance, more usually a vehicle for the bare simplicity of his thought than for beauty of phrase. Therefore they are sometimes more rugged than easy, more difficult than comprehensible. Yet Emerson occupies a secure place as an American poet; and his range is wide, from the childlike humor of "The Mountain and the Squirrel," through the pure beauty of "The Rhodora," to the cryptic obscurity of his "Brahma." In the latter appears a nugget of what is called Emerson's transcendentalism, the uplifting thought that over us all is a spirit which will strengthen and lead us. This is given more concisely still in the two lines upon his tombstone, which express the spiritual aim of Emerson's whole life and achievement:

The passive master lent his hand
To the vast soul which o'er him planned.

A proof of the depth of Emerson's wisdom was that he allied himself with but one of the new movements of his day. America was full of enthusiasts and prophets, mystics,

founders of experiments in social living. They flocked to Emerson's door; he saw the weaknesses of their ideas, yet he was very patient with them. He would not join with them, however. He did not go to Brook Farm, as Hawthorne did; nor would he take part in Alcott's Fruitlands. He went his way alone, except that upon due deliberation he supported the growing abolitionism. Yet he would not share its extremes nor its violence. He gave to it his ideas, and they gradually made their way.

Conservative Concord, though from the first it respected Emerson, was slow in following him. Said one prominent citizen to him, early in the slavery controversy, "There are only three persons, as far as I know, whose opinions are obnoxious to the members of our community: they are, Theodore Parker, Wendell Phillips, and—if I may be so candid—yourself, Sir." But Concord eventually followed and supported him. And personally he was always respected and beloved. The town knew him in all his transparent ways, whether working in his garden; or walking in the streets and fields and woods; or sitting in silence at town meetings, where he admired the rugged eloquence of the speakers; or beating down with his cane a sign insulting the town doctor, advocate of temperance, which drinkers had hung upon the Milldam. Emerson had no concealments, no politics, no hesitation to speak his mind, no superiority to the simpler people around him. He was no crank, no unbalanced reformer. Gentle in manner, plain in dress, unaffected in all his ways, a true neighbor, he was yet known to be inflexible in principle and fearless of all entrenched conservatism that opposed (but so vainly) the innovations of his thought.

Emerson's life in Concord was that of a plain citizen, claiming nothing from his acknowledged eminence. He was never aloof, as was Hawthorne in his way, or Thoreau in his. Emerson served on committees. He had a strange regret for the scholarliness which he could not put off, and which barred him from the impromptu forum of the blacksmith shop or the street corner. His townsmen he always respected, and he envied practical ability wherever he saw it. Wrote he: "I like people who can do things. When Edward and I struggled in vain to drag our big calf into the barn, the Irish girl put her finger in the calf's mouth and led her in directly." By the same token Emerson was a poor gardener and clumsy with tools. His little boy said to him, "Papa, I'm afraid you'll dig your leg." A committee of the Horticultural Society called upon him to see the soil which produced such poor specimens of such fine varieties. Emerson was amused at his own limitations, admitted them, and perceived their warning. "I stoop to pull up a weed that is choking the corn, and find there are two; close behind is a third; behind that there are four thousand and one. I am heated and untuned." He concluded, "The scholar shall not dig."

But if gardening tired him and unfitted him for the study, walking did not. Though slender and apparently frail, he was a tireless walker, and found in the woods and fields stimulus for thought. The farmers knew that he respected them; on their ground he was a learner.

On the other hand, when he spoke to them from the Lyceum platform he gave them his best, never speaking down to them. One farmer claimed to have heard all of Mr. Emerson's lectures, and added, "And understood 'em too." A Concord workwoman, helping at Madam Hoar's, went home early one afternoon: she was going to Mr. Emerson's lecture. Asked if she understood him, she answered, "Not a word, but I like to go and see him stand up there and look as if he thought everyone was as good as he was."

The only unkind action toward Emerson in his town was effectually checked. A neighbor sought to blackmail him by moving an ugly old shed into the lot before his house. In the night a number of young men, provided with ropes, hooks, and a ladder, came and pulled the old thing down. They were never named; but Emerson's son, writing of this many years afterward, implied that it was perfectly known who they were.

And when his house caught fire, never was neighborly help more complete in saving books, papers, and furniture, and in putting out the fire. The excitement and exposure of

Emerson's Study, now in the Concord Museum

the incident threatened Emerson's health; but his neighbors and friends combined to send him abroad and repair the building. He went to Europe and Egypt with his daughter, recruited his strength, and when he returned was welcomed by his townspeople, who led him, under a triumphal arch, to the restored house. At first believing that the welcome was to his daughter, at last he perceived its meaning, and going back to the gate, said to them all, "My friends, I know that this is not a tribute to an old man and his daughter returned to their house, but to the common blood of us all—one family—in Concord!"

Emerson died, enfeebled by age, in 1882, and was buried in Sleepy Hollow Cemetery, where others of his name lie around him.

BRONSON ALCOTT

It was in 1840 that Amos Bronson Alcott, drawn by his friendship with Emerson, came to Concord and lived in the Hosmer Cottage far out on Main Street. Here soon afterward was born the last of his four daughters. Alcott, born in Connecticut in 1799, once a peddler and tutor in the South, and but lately the owner of the unsuccessful Temple School in Boston, was a reformer in education, a writer whose first book remained largely unsold, and a philosopher whose *Conversations with Children on the Gospels* had brought him something of fame but little in money. So poor was he and unpretentious in his ways that he began in Concord, besides tilling his own garden, as a day laborer in the fields. In the winter that followed he chopped wood in Concord woodlots for a dollar a day. As he grew poorer, he did much of the housework; and from clothes handed down to his daughters he designed and cut dresses for them. But in 1842, on Emerson's money, he went to England to see unknown friends who admired him through his writings, and returned bringing the Englishman Charles Lane, and the idea of setting up a new venture in living, philosophical, vegetarian—and sadly impractical. It was begun at Fruitlands in the town of Harvard in 1843,

Orchard House, Home of the Alcotts

and after but a single season came to complete failure. Alcott's disappointment and disillusion were so great that he wished to die; but nature was too strong. In 1844, again with Emerson's help, he returned to Concord, and the next year moved into the house on Lexington Road which he called Hillside, later to become Hawthorne's Wayside. By planting and hard labor he improved the place within and without, and lived there several years.

Emerson wrote of Alcott, "He is a great man. . . . His conversation is sublime. . . . Yet when I see how he is underestimated by cultivated people, I fancy none but I have heard him talk." But perhaps Emerson gave Alcott an inspiration that no one else could supply. At any rate, Concord, and the wider world of his day, never understood Alcott—and he took a deal of understanding. He never learned the value of money, and his wife and children carried many cares of which he seemed unaware. Unpractical, though a hard worker with his hands, according to all worldly standards he was improvident, depending as he did upon the guidance of one higher than himself. His books brought him little money; his lecture tours brought him almost less, for from one he returned with but a dollar in cash. The help of Emerson tided him through his worst period. Yet the Sage of Concord was serene and untroubled among difficulties which he hardly perceived. His trust in Providence was sublime: once it all but confounded his loving but doubting family. On a snowy winter's night, when characteristically the supply of wood was very low, a neighbor's child came and begged fuel, for there was a baby in the house, and no money. Mrs. Alcott hesitated: she also had a baby. But Alcott said, "Give half our stock. The weather will moderate, or wood will come." The wood was given, but the weather grew worse, and at bedtime the Alcotts were about to cover their fire to keep it, when a farmer knocked at the door. He had started for Boston with a load of wood, but the drifts were so bad that he asked if he might not drop the wood in the Alcotts' yard. Alcott might pay for it at any time. The family was deeply impressed; the incident seemed to justify one of Mrs. Alcott's sayings:

"Cast your bread upon the waters, and after many days it will come back buttered."

With providential and with neighborly care Alcott plodded on. A certain amount of recognition came to him, very comforting when Concord, recognizing at last the worth of his educational ideas, made him superintendent of its schools. But he was always idealistic and impractical, as his daughter once humorously indicated. He had at length set up in Concord his longed-for School of Philosophy, which in its short life caused a pleasant flutter among the many theorists of the day. Miss Alcott, being asked to define a philosopher, said that he was a man up in a balloon, with his family holding to the ropes and trying to haul him back to earth.

Fortunately this very daughter Louisa held the strongest rope. She never hauled him down; but she sent up ample supplies, so that he and his fellow dreamers could hover above the earth in comfort. Her story is one of real heroism.

LOUISA ALCOTT

Louisa May Alcott was in 1832 born into this family where everything revolved around the father, and where hardship was cheerfully borne because of the ideals which he taught and lived up to. He was almost her only teacher; but he wisely encouraged on the one hand the romping which made her strong in youth, and on the other the play of fancy by which she came to live. Her attitude toward him was tenderly protective. For need of money she helped out at home and tried domestic service; but from first to last she stuck to her writing. She had some small success with the magazines. She went to the Civil War as a nurse, caught typhoid pneumonia, and though she survived it, it was at the cost of her health. She said that she had never been ill before, and never well afterward.

But with inborn courage and persistence, she continued her work. A publisher advised her to teach; but she answered that she would not—she would prove that she could write. Her *Hospital Sketches* of her Civil War experiences had some success; but *Moods,* her first novel, was not profitable. Then another publisher asked her to write a girls' book. She answered, "I'll try." The result was *Little Women.*

The success of this book made her reputation and the family fortune. Other books followed, very popular in their day, and still read in ours. Yet they are, almost without exception, juvenile fiction. Only *Little Women* reaches up to the full stature of a novel. Its portrayal of the humors of the childhood of the Alcott sisters, their difficulties and struggles on reaching maturity, the tragedy of a death, and the romance of three marriages, has pleased and touched generations of readers. No book written in Concord (it was, however, but partly written in the Orchard House) has had such a vogue or such financial success. The Alcott family burden was lifted. The father took it placidly, as he took everything. And Louisa continued writing.

The story of Louisa Alcott is, therefore, one of dogged courage triumphant over difficulties. Not great as a stylist or a thinker, she knew how to reach the heart. Few have more deserved success. It should be better known that she wrote two touching poems: one on Thoreau's death ("Thoreau's Flute") and one to her aged and helpless father. He died on the fourth of March 1888, she but two days later. Both lie buried in Sleepy Hollow.

The oldest sister, Anna, married and lived in Concord. A measure of artistic success and fame came to the youngest, May. She was the first teacher of Daniel Chester French, the sculptor, and in her own right a good painter, though best known for her copies of Turner. She married and lived abroad; but her youthful drawings on the walls of Orchard House are well known to tourists.

THOREAU

Another Concord writer, competing in fame with Emerson, is Henry David Thoreau. His still growing reputation amounts, with some students, almost to a cult. He was a prophet of individualism, a student of nature, a writer whose method of life and subject matter set him apart from all others. The comparison of him with Emerson is inevitable: their habits of work were the same, in producing books culled from voluminous journals. Alcott did the like, to be sure; but his books are pale and spineless compared with Emerson's, and even Emerson's lack the vigor of Thoreau. In the latter's essays he touches upon Emerson's ground, not always to his own advantage. But Thoreau was no imitator, except in his early unconscious following of more mature thought. Least of all did he imitate anyone in his particular field of writing or in his way of life.

Of this last it has been humorously said that it is popularly believed that Thoreau spent half of his life in Concord jail and half in Walden woods. The germ of truth in this is that he spent practically all of his life in Concord. His travels were brief; his longest stay was a year spent in tutoring on Staten Island, from which he was glad to return. But he said of himself, "I have travelled a good deal in Concord." And though his neighbors considered him idle, the reality is a life of steady purpose in developing his own genius. This was as peculiar as that of any American writer, yet resulted in a permanent source of inspiration to many since his day.

Thoreau was born in 1817 in a house on the Virginia Road; he was christened David Henry, a sequence which he later reversed. He went to school in Concord and to college at Harvard, and began life as teacher in the Concord public school. But Deacon Ball objected to the absence of whipping, whereupon Thoreau whipped half a dozen pupils in one afternoon and then resigned as a teacher. He then set up a school with his brother John, to whom he was devoted. But John died suddenly of lockjaw, a terrible blow to Henry. He lived then for awhile in the Emerson household, in which at other periods he was a member of the family. Clever with his hands as few others were, he was useful about the place, practical helper in all household matters, and companion and friend to the children.

In 1845, following a plan which he had long had in his mind, Thoreau built himself a hut (pp. 36-37) on Emerson's land at Walden Pond, and lived there for a little more than two years. His time he spent wandering in the woods, writing in his journal, and completing the manuscript of his *A Week on the Concord and Merrimack Rivers,* the half-philosophic journal of a trip taken some years earlier with his brother. Finding no publisher, he brought out the work at his own expense, and later had to store at home in the village the unsold copies. He had now a library, he said, of a thousand volumes, over seven hundred of which he had written himself. It was not until 1854 that he brought out *Walden,* a book arising from his experiences at the pond, and on which, to most people, his fame rests. It is a very personal and direct account of his life there, with a semi-narrative quality impossible to Emerson. It is in fact the personal quality of his work that gives Thoreau's writings their force and interest, while Emerson's personality lies hidden.

There is, however, one more quality to the book (and to the best of Thoreau's writings) which gives it its timelessness. That is its social gospel—the need of each soul to depend upon itself, and to break free of the shackles of human conventions and ancient institutions. This scorn of what others accepted is more prominent still in his "A Plea for Captain John Brown," and his "On the Duty of 'Civil Disobedience'," the latter said to have been in great part the inspiration of Gandhi.

Thoreau published no other works than these in his lifetime, except for a few more essays and speeches. Much was published after his death, however, including his many journals. Necessary to his life at home, after Walden, were his wide wanderings in the town and in fact in the region. If he wanted to go anywhere he would strike across country afoot. His costume was unconventional, his manners abrupt; to strangers he was crusty, and even to his friends he was, as Emerson said, "with difficulty, sweet." Yet he had a few close friends, the poet Channing, Emerson himself, Alcott, and others less known. In his own fashion he let people see how little he cared for their ways. In protest against the Mexican War he refused to pay his poll tax, and therefore was put in jail. But the stay was for a single night, as his aunt paid the tax, and he was set free.

Thoreau never married. His youthful love affair with Ellen Sewall (who refused both brothers) was short and on his part transcendentally lofty. She cannot have understood him, and he was not easy to understand. Disappointed though he may have been, he had no self-pity. And viewed at this distance, a married Thoreau seems impossible. If for a time the dream seemed to lure him from his course, the vision faded. The experience threw him still further back into himself, and he went his strange way, free of all such ties.

Thoreau was mistaken in his claim that he was independent of society, that he lived on the few beans that he raised at Walden, or on the few dollars that later he chose to earn yearly. He squatted on Emerson's land; before and afterward he lived with his parents and sisters. Money for his personal needs he earned by lecturing (at which he never was a success), by surveying or by carpentering, or in his father's pencil factory. It is not true that when he had learned to make a perfect pencil he gave up making more; the truth was that his improved method of making graphite was more profitable and drove the other business out. Nevertheless, while Thoreau was more dependent on society at large than he cared to acknowledge, in all his ways he was aloof. He simplified his life. In Concord affairs he took no part except when he lectured at the Lyceum, or when in his indignation at the fate of John Brown he called the town together to listen to his "Plea." A timorous friend advised him to give up the plan. He replied that there was to be a meeting, and that he would speak. His courage, in large ways like this when public opinion was against him, or in the small ways of manners and daily life, was not to be questioned. The force of his example and the power of his words have inspired many to follow him in breaking free from the minor absurdities of custom or the great injustices of a complacent society. And in these ways he is still a force.

Perhaps the intensity with which he lived his life, thought his thoughts, and expressed them in his striking fashion wore down the oaken strength which Emerson admired. He was reckless of exposure, and a cold gave way to consumption. As he lay dying in his Main Street house, a relative ventured to ask him if he had made his peace with God. The independent, free in religion as in everything else, replied, "I didn't know that we had ever quarrelled, Aunt." He died in 1862, and, like the others of whom we have written here, lies on the ridge in Sleepy Hollow.

HAWTHORNE

Nathaniel Hawthorne, more of an outsider than all the rest, more solitary in Concord streets than Thoreau at Walden, is yet more identified with Concord than with any other of his various residences. Born in Salem in 1804, he lived in his youth the life of a recluse even in his own home, and emerged only gradually into the outer world. Always a writer, but without marked early success, he spent a year at the idealistic Brook Farm. Then marrying, he brought his bride to Concord in 1842, to live three years in the house which, following the title he gave the book that he wrote there (*Mosses from an Old Manse*), has ever since been called the Old Manse. But the book failed to remove the pressure of necessity; for the needs of his family he accepted an appointment at the Salem Customs House, and so in 1845 brought to an end his first Concord period.

In spite of the need of money, however, his life in the Manse was idyllic. Thoroughly happy in his wife, he desired no other human companionship, would sometimes flee when strangers appeared, and once when his wife was away for two days he took pride in speaking to no one, not even the servant. He worked in his garden before the house, and often was seen standing long periods in meditation, leaning upon his hoe. He walked to the village

The Old Manse

for his mail, shy of all that he met. And he wandered in the fields, or rowed on the river in the boat which he bought from Thoreau, sometimes with Thoreau himself.

For he was ready to receive certain friends who had secured his approval. Emerson would come, and Channing the poet, and Thoreau, whose silence was like Hawthorne's own. Margaret Fuller was an occasional visitor. Also there came friends from other places, such as Franklin Pierce, not yet president. Hawthorne was constant in his affections, though closest of all to his heart was his love for his wife and children.

In 1852 Hawthorne returned again to Concord. His novels (*The Scarlet Letter, The House of the Seven Gables,* and *The Blithedale Romance*) had brought him success. In the *Romance,* the scene of the searching for the body of the drowned Zenobia was drawn from an incident in Concord itself. More prosperous now, Hawthorne bought Alcott's Hillside, named it Wayside, and fitted it for his occupancy. Here he collected some of his earlier stories, and wrote *Tanglewood Tales.* Here also, at the request of Franklin Pierce, then campaigning for the presidency, he wrote for him a campaign biography.

Although no longer so great a recluse, Hawthorne was still shy. He spent long hours meditating on the ridge behind his house, and when descending, Alcott said, "if he caught sight of any one in the road he would go under cover like a partridge." He knew the town so little that when the Emerson children showed him pictures of the Square and the Milldam he asked where they were.

When Pierce was elected president he offered Hawthorne the consulship at Liverpool. After but a year at Concord, therefore, Hawthorne went away again, to stay abroad seven years. He traveled on the continent, made with his *Marble Faun* still more success, and returned in 1860 almost a man of the world. In company he now met people readily; yet he would withdraw himself, to meditate on the problems which burdened him. The charge that he was gloomy, at least in the subjects of his stories, was always denied by his worshiping wife. He was, she said, "like a stray Seraph, who had experienced in his life no evil, but . . . saw and sorrowed over evil."

If we accept that explanation, his vision and his sorrow overcame him in the last few years of his life. The Civil War oppressed him, some physical cause also may have sapped his strength, and he could do no steady work. In the tower which he built on top of Wayside, where he could be safe from interruption, or in meditating long upon his ridge, he could not bring to a satisfactory end the four separate novels which he tried to write. His mysterious burdens were too great. At length, going away with Pierce for a vacation in New Hampshire, he died in his sleep on the night of the eighteenth-nineteenth of May 1864. His body was brought back to Concord, and he lies buried near his famous friends.

Other Writers. Emerson, the Alcotts, Thoreau, and Hawthorne are the group on whom the literary fame of Concord will most securely rest. Other well-known writers have lived in Concord for longer or shorter periods, notably Margaret Fuller, George William Curtis, the younger William Ellery Channing (the poet), Franklin B. Sanborn, and Jane Austin, the American historical novelist. Here lived also Mrs. Daniel Lothrop (Margaret Sidney), author of the "Five Little Peppers" books (pp. 44–45). But these are either less in fame or of a later time. We stop, chronologically, with the death of the Alcotts, and leave to a later or a larger book the many facts and anecdotes about those who, in this or other fields of endeavor, have added to the reputation of Concord.

The Emerson House

Bibliography

HISTORICAL

Many of these works are out of print, but are worth seeking in public libraries. Some have been reprinted in facsimile or in paperback editions.

BROOKS, PAUL. *The View from Lincoln Hill.* Houghton Mifflin Company, 1976.

BROWN, LOUISE K. *Wilderness Town, The Story of Bedford, Massachusetts.* Privately printed, 1968.

CHAMBERLAIN SAMUEL, and STEWART BEACH. *Lexington and Concord in Color.* Hastings House, 1970.

COBURN, FRANK WARREN. *The Battle of April 19, 1775.* 2d ed. Lexington Historical Society, 1922.

EMERSON, AMELIA FORBES, ed. *Diaries and Letters of William Emerson, 1743 - 1776.* Privately printed, n.d. [1972].

EMERSON, RALPH WALDO. "Bi-Centennial Address" [1835]. In *Miscellanies.* Complete Works. Centenary Edition.

FENN, MARY R. *Old Houses of Concord.* Old Concord Chapter, D.A.R., 1974.

FRENCH, ALLEN. *Old Concord.* Little, Brown & Company, 1915.

———. *The Day of Concord and Lexington.* Little, Brown & Company, 1925.

————. *General Gage's Informers.* University of Michigan Press, 1932.

GROSS, ROBERT A., *The Minutemen and Their World.* Hill and Wang, 1976.

HUDSON, CHARLES. *History of the Town of Lexington.* Wiggin & Lunt, 1868.

The Lexington-Concord Battle Road. Interim Report of the Boston National Historic Sites Commission to the Congress of the United States, June 16, 1958. U.S. Government Printing Office, 1959.

LITTLE, DAVID B. *America's First Centennial Celebration.* 2d ed. Houghton Mifflin Company, 1974.

MURDOCK, HAROLD. *The Nineteenth of April, 1775.* Houghton Mifflin Company, 1923.

PHALEN, HAROLD R. *History of the Town of Acton.* Privately printed, 1954.

RICHARDSON, LAURENCE EATON. *Concord River.* Barre Publishers, 1964.

RUSSELL, FRANCIS. *Lexington, Concord, and Bunker Hill.* American Heritage Junior Library, 1963.

SCUDDER, TOWNSEND. *Concord: American Town.* Little, Brown & Company, 1947.

SHATTUCK, LEMUEL. *History of the Town of Concord.* Russell, Odiorne & Co., 1835. Facsimile edition distributed by Goodspeed's Book Shop, 18 Beacon Street, Boston, Mass. 02108.

TOURTELLOT, ARTHUR BERNON. *William Diamond's Drum.* Doubleday & Company, Inc., 1959; reprint ed. W. W. Norton, 1963, as *Lexington and Concord: The Beginning of the War of the American Revolution.*

WALCOTT, CHARLES H. *Concord in the Colonial Period.* Estes and Lauriat, 1884.

WHEELER, RUTH R. *Concord: Climate for Freedom.* The Concord Antiquarian Society, 1967.

WILKINS, RUTH CHAMBERLIN. *Carlisle, Its History and Heritage.* Carlisle Historical Society, Inc., 1976.

BIBLIOGRAPHY

LITERARY

One should read the great writers themselves as well as books about them. As a taste at first hand from each, the following are suggested.

EMERSON. The best complete edition is the Centenary (Houghton Mifflin Company), twelve volumes, with ten from the *Journals.* Read at least *Nature* (not the essay but the complete book); the first and second series of *Essays, The Conduct of Life, Representative Men.* In the poems read at least "Good-Bye," "Each and All," "The Problem," "Hamatreya," "The Rhodora," "Woodnotes," "Musketaquid," "Concord Hymn," "Brahma."

There are, however, shorter editions of Emerson, considerably reduced. The "Libraries," such as Everyman's, Modern Library, the World's Classics, and the American Writers' Series, have excellent volumes of selections, sometimes with valuable introductory essays.

Selections from the *Journals* are collected into *The Heart of Emerson's Journals,* edited by Bliss Perry. Houghton Mifflin Company, 1926.

THOREAU. The best collected edition is *The Writings of Henry David Thoreau,* 1906, twenty volumes including the *Journals.* But as with Emerson (above) there are various collections in the different "Libraries." Most of these contain *Walden* complete. This should be read in any case, with parts of *Cape Cod* and *The Maine Woods,* and the essays "A Plea for Captain John Brown," "Civil Disobedience" (originally called "Resistance to Civil Government"), and "Walking." The *Journals* are very long, but are condensed in *The Heart of Thoreau's Journals,* edited by Odell Shepard, 1927. *Men of Concord,* selected by Francis H. Allen, and finely illustrated by N. C. Wyeth, is excellent, 1936. (All these are published by Houghton Mifflin Company.)

ALCOTT, BRONSON. His original volumes are hard reading nowadays. Better is *The Journals of Bronson Alcott,* edited by Odell Shepard (Little, Brown & Company), 1938.

ALCOTT, LOUISA. Her best book is *Little Women*, in various editions. Others do not reach up to the same stature; but *An Old-Fashioned Girl* and *Little Men* are good reading.

HAWTHORNE. His best are perhaps *The Scarlet Letter, The Marble Faun, The House of the Seven Gables,* and such collections as *Mosses from an Old Manse,* the preface of which tells of his Concord life. The *Journals* are best found in *The Heart of Hawthorne's Journals,* edited by Newton Arvin (Houghton Mifflin Company), 1929. More complete are the *American Notebooks* and the *English Notebooks,* edited by Randall Stewart (Yale University Press), 1933 and 1941.

BIOGRAPHICAL

BROOKS, VAN WYCK. *The Flowering of New England.* Dutton, 1936. Places the writers in relation to each other and to their time.

MATTHIESSEN, F. O. *American Renaissance. Art and Expression in the Age of Emerson and Whitman.* Oxford University Press, 1941. A much more abstruse study.

EMERSON

BROOKS, VAN WYCK. *The Life of Emerson.* Dutton, 1932.

CABOT, JAMES ELLIOT. *A Memoir of Ralph Waldo Emerson.* Houghton Mifflin Company, 1887.

EMERSON, EDWARD WALDO. *Emerson in Concord.* Houghton Mifflin Company, 1889.

RUSK, RALPH L. *The Life of Ralph Waldo Emerson.* Charles Scribner's Sons, 1949.

THOREAU

BAZALGETTE, LEON. *Henry Thoreau, Bachelor of Nature.*

Translated by Van Wyck Brooks. Harcourt Brace and Co., 1924.

CANBY, HENRY SEIDEL. *Thoreau.* Houghton Mifflin Company, 1939.

CHANNING, WILLIAM E. *Thoreau the Poet Naturalist.* Goodspeed, 1902.

HARDING, WALTER. *The Days of Henry Thoreau.* Alfred A. Knopf, 1965.

SALT, HENRY S. *Life of Henry David Thoreau.* London: Scott, 1906.

VAN DOREN, MARK. *Henry David Thoreau.* Houghton Mifflin Company, 1916.

ALCOTT, AMOS BRONSON

SANBORN F. B., and W. T. HARRIS. *A. Bronson Alcott, His Life and Philosophy.* Roberts, 1893.

SHEPARD, ODELL. *Pedlar's Progress.* Little, Brown & Company, 1937.

ALCOTT, LOUISA MAY

BRADFORD, GAMALIEL. Essay in *Portraits of American Women.* Houghton Mifflin Company, 1919. Also contains an essay on Sarah Ripley.

CHENEY, MRS. E. D. L. *Louisa May Alcott, Her Life, Letters, and Journals.* Little, Brown & Company, 1911.

HAWTHORNE

ARVIN, NEWTON. *Hawthorne.* London: Douglas, 1930.

HAWTHORNE, JULIAN. *Nathaniel Hawthorne and His Wife.* Houghton Mifflin Company, 1884.

———. *Hawthorne and His Circle.* Harper and Brothers, 1903.

LATHROP, ROSE HAWTHORNE. *Memories of Hawthorne.* Houghton Mifflin Company, 1897.

Index

Acton company of Minute
  Men, 9, 65, 66, 68
Adams, Samuel, 5, 38, 56, 57
Alarm company, 54, 66
Alcott, Amos Bronson, 44,
  80-83
Alcott, Louisa May, 29, 42,
  83-84
Alcott family, 27, 29, 34, 42
Andros, Governor, 12, 52, 72
Apple Slump, 42
Arlington Historical Society,
  Introductory Note
Assabet River, 26, 49

Ball, Nehemiah, 26, 85
Barrett, James, 16, 26-27, 54,
  64-66
Barrett, Thomas, 27, 62
Barrett's Mill, 27
Barrett's Mill Road, 26, 27
Battle Road, 3, 8, 9
Battle Road Visitor Center, 1
Battleground, 20-25
Bedford Street, 27
Belknap Street, 34
Bliss, Daniel, 17
Bloody Angle, 9-10
Boston National Historic Sites
  Commission, Introductory
  Note
Brewster, William, 25, 31
Brister's Hill, 35
Brook Farm, 77, 88
Brown, John, 33, 38, 86, 87

Brown, Reuben, 38, 41, 60, 64
Buckman Tavern, 4, 57
Bulkeley, Edward, 52
Bulkeley, Peter, 15, 26, 50, 51
Bull, Ephraim Wales, 30, 46
Buttrick, John, 16, 25, 54, 60,
  65, 66, 68

Cambridge Turnpike, 12
Cary Memorial Building, 6
Catholic Church, St. Bernard's,
  27
Channing, William Ellery, 28,
  33, 74, 87, 90, 91
Christian Science Church, 26
Clarke, Jonas, 56
College Lane, 71
Colonial Inn, 12, 13
Concord Academy, 33
Concord Antiquarian Society,
  see Concord Museum
Concord Art Association, 38
Concord-Carlisle Regional
  High School, 35
Concord Fight, 65-72
Concord Free Public Library,
  32-33
Concord grape, 30, 46
Concord Museum, 12, 24,
  40-41
Concord River, 23, 49
Concord, the name of, 51

Davis, Isaac, 24, 66, 68
Dawes, William, 55

[99   ]

Dawn of Liberty, 6
Diorama of Concord Fight, 24
Doolittle, Amos, 6, plate insert
Dovecote, 34

Earl, Ralph, plate insert
Egg Rock, 26
Elm Street, 33
Emerson, Mary Moody, 29-30, 74
Emerson, Ralph Waldo, Introductory Note, 16, 19, 28-30, 38, 40, 74-80
Emerson, William, 16, 18, 38, 61-62, 68, 73
Emerson house, 40
Everett, Edward, 4

Felton, Septimius, 45, 69
Fenn School, 25
First Parish Church in Concord, 38, 71, 87
First Parish Church in Lexington, 3, 59
Fiske, Lieut. Ebenezer, farmhouse, 9
Fiske, Hill, xiii, 8
French, Daniel Chester, 24, 25, 28, 84
Fruitlands, 77, 80
Fuller, Margaret, 28, 74, 90

Grapevine Cottage, 46
Graves of British soldiers, 21, 22
Great Meadows National Wildlife Refuge, 30-31
Gunflints, 26, 65

Hancock, John, 5, 38, 56, 57
Hancock-Clarke house, 5, 56
Hapgood Wright Town Forest, 35
Harrington, Jonathan, 5, 59
Harvard College, 71
Hawthorne, Nathaniel, 19, 28-29, 44, 88-91

Hawthorne, Mrs. Nathaniel, 20, 29, 88
Hayward, James, 9
Heywood house, 38, 40
Hildreth's Corner, 27
Hill Burying Ground, 15-17
Hillside, 44, 82, 90
Hiram Lodge of Freemasons, 7
Hoar, John, 42, 52
Hoar, Samuel (Squire), 30
Hoar family, 30
Hosmer, Abner, 24
Hosmer, Joseph, 26, 34, 61, 65, 66
Hosmer cottage, 34, 80
House with the Bullet Hole, 18, 62

Indians, 49-52

Jack, John, 17
Jason Russell house, Introduction
Jethro's Tree, 12, 15, 20
Jones, Elisha, 18, 61-62, 70
Jones, John, 50, 51

King Philip, 51
Kitson, Henry H., 3

Laurie, Captain, 23, 65, 66, 68
Lexington, Battle of, 58-60
Lexington Green, 3, 56-60
Lexington Historical Society, Introduction, 4, 5, 6, 9
Lexington Minute Men, 7, 56-60
Lexington Road, 38, 61
Lexington Visitors Center, 5
Liberty Pole, 62
Liberty Street, 25, 26
Little Women, 34, 42, 84
Loring N. Fowler Memorial Library, 32
Lothrop, Mrs. Daniel, 29, 44-45

INDEX

Lowell Road, 26
Lyceums, 75, 78, 87

Main Street, 31
Main Street Burying Ground, 32
Melvin Memorial, 28, 72
Menotomy, 58
Meriam's Corner, 46-47, 61, 70
Middlesex School, 27
Milldam, 12, 31
Mill pond, 31
Minute Man National Historical Park, Introductory Note, 1, 25
Minute Man statue, Concord, 24-25
Minute Man statue, Lexington, 3
Minute Men, 7, 54
Monsen Road, 30
Monument Square, 11-17
Monument Street, 17
Moulton, Martha, 64
Munroe Tavern, 6-7
Museum of Our National Heritage, 8

Nature, 19, 41, 75
Nineteenths of April, 53, 72
North Bridge, 20-24, 64
North Bridge Visitor Center, 25

Old Calf Pasture, 26
Old Manse, 18-20, 24, 62, 73, 74, 88
Orchard House, 42, 52, 84

Parker, John, 4, 56-59
Parker, Jonas, 5, 59
Parsons, Captain, 21, 23, 64, 66, 70
Percy, Lord, 6, 7, 71
Pierce, Franklin, 45, 90, 91
Pitcairn, Maj. John, 4, 15, 57, 62, 64

Prescott, Samuel, 56, 60
Prichard Gate, 28
Provincial Congress, 38, 53, 56
Punkatasset Hill, 25, 65

Red Bridge, 26
Revere, Paul, 5, 9, 12, 55-56
Revolutionary Monument, Lexington, 4-5
Revolutionary Monument of 1836, 21
Ridge path, Sleepy Hollow, 28-30
Ripley, Ezra, 19
Ripley, Samuel and Sarah, 19
River Street, 34
Rivers, 49
Robbins, Roland Wells, 36
Robinson, John, 66

Sanborn, Franklin B., 28, 33, 91
Sanderson house, 7
Sandham, Henry, 6
School of Philosophy, 44, 83
Sewall, Ellen, 87
Shattuck, Job, 12, 13, 71
Shepard, Mary, 51
Sidney, Margaret, *see* Lothrop, Mrs. Daniel
Smith, Lieut. Col. Francis, 15, 57, 62, 64, 69, 71
Sleepy Hollow Cemetery, 28-30, 80, 84, 88, 91
South Bridge, 34, 64
South Bridge Boat House, 34
Sudbury River, 26, 49
Sutherland, Lieutenant, 24, 58, 66, 68

Tenth Regiment, 57
Texas, 34
Thoreau, Henry D., 29, 31, 38, 47, 84-88
Thoreau, John, 13
Thoreau, John (the son), 85
Thoreau-Alcott house, 33, 88

Thoreau Lyceum, 34-35
Thoreau Street, 34
Thoreau Texas house, 34-35
Town House, 15, 27, 64
Transcendentalism, 44, 76
Trustees of Reservations, 20

Virginia Road, 47, 85

Walden, 35-37, 86
Walden Pond, 35-37
Walden Street, 34, 38

War monuments, Concord, 13, 72
Washington, President, 7
Wayside, 44, 82, 90
Wheeler, Thomas, 51
Wheeler, Timothy, 62
White, Deacon, 13
Whitney, Samuel, 44
Willard, Simon, 50, 52
Wright Tavern, 12, 15, 38, 62-63